Turning towards the Lord

U. M. LANG
OF THE ORATORY

Turning towards the Lord

Orientation in Liturgical Prayer

IGNATIUS PRESS   SAN FRANCISCO

Cover art:
Apse mosaic, depicting the Tree of Life
Basilica of San Clemente, Rome
Scala/Art Resource, New York

Cover design by Roxanne Mei Lum

ISBN 0–89870–986–5
Library of Congress Control Number 2003115824
Printed in the United States of America ∞

To the memory of
Father Michael Napier of the Oratory

CONTENTS

FOREWORD

To the ordinary churchgoer, the two most obvious effects of the liturgical reform of the Second Vatican Council seem to be the disappearance of Latin and the turning of the altars towards the people. Those who read the relevant texts will be astonished to learn that neither is in fact found in the decrees of the Council. The use of the vernacular is certainly permitted, especially for the Liturgy of the Word, but the preceding general rule of the Council text says, 'Particular law remaining in force, the use of the Latin language is to be preserved in the Latin rites' (*Sacrosanctum Concilium*, 36.1). There is nothing in the Council text about turning altars towards the people; that point is raised only in post-conciliar instructions. The most important directive is found in paragraph 262 of the *Institutio Generalis Missalis Romani*, the General Instruction of the new Roman Missal, issued in 1969. That says, 'It is better for the main altar to be constructed away from the wall so that one can easily walk around the altar and celebrate facing the people (*versus populum*).' The General Instruction of the Missal issued in 2002 retained this text unaltered except for the addition of the subordinate clause, 'which is desirable wherever possible'. This was taken in many quarters as hardening the 1969 text to mean that there was now a general obligation to set up altars facing the people 'wherever possible'. This interpretation, however, was rejected by the Congregation for Divine Worship on 25 September 2000, when it declared that the word '*expedit*' ('is desirable') did not imply an obligation but only

9

made a suggestion. The physical orientation, the Congregation says, must be distinguished from the spiritual. Even if a priest celebrates *versus populum*, he should always be oriented *versus Deum per Iesum Christum* (towards God through Jesus Christ). Rites, signs, symbols, and words can never exhaust the inner reality of the mystery of salvation. For this reason the Congregation warns against one-sided and rigid positions in this debate.

This is an important clarification. It sheds light on what is relative in the external symbolic forms of the liturgy and resists the fanaticisms that, unfortunately, have not been uncommon in the controversies of the last forty years. At the same time it highlights the internal direction of liturgical action, which can never be expressed in its totality by external forms. This internal direction is the same for priest and people, towards the Lord—towards the Father through Christ in the Holy Spirit. The Congregation's response should thus make for a new, more relaxed discussion, in which we can search for the best ways of putting into practice the mystery of salvation. The quest is to be achieved, not by condemning one another, but by carefully listening to each other and, even more importantly, listening to the internal guidance of the liturgy itself. The labelling of positions as 'preconciliar', 'reactionary', and 'conservative', or as 'progressive' and 'alien to the faith' achieves nothing; what is needed is a new mutual openness in the search for the best realisation of the memorial of Christ.

This small book by Uwe Michael Lang, a member of the London Oratory, studies the direction of liturgical prayer from a historical, theological, and pastoral point of view. At a propitious moment, as it seems to me, this book resumes a debate that, despite appearances to the contrary, has never really gone away, not even after the Second Vatican Council. The

Innsbruck liturgist Josef Andreas Jungmann, one of the architects of the Council's Constitution on the Sacred Liturgy, was from the very beginning resolutely opposed to the polemical catchphrase that previously the priest celebrated 'with his back to the people'; he emphasised that what was at issue was not the priest turning away from the people, but, on the contrary, his facing the same direction as the people. The Liturgy of the Word has the character of proclamation and dialogue, to which address and response can rightly belong. But in the Liturgy of the Eucharist the priest leads the people in prayer and is turned, together with the people, towards the Lord. For this reason, Jungmann argued, the common direction of priest and people is intrinsically fitting and proper to the liturgical action. Louis Bouyer (like Jungmann, one of the Council's leading liturgists) and Klaus Gamber have each in his own way taken up the same question. Despite their great reputations, they were unable to make their voices heard at first, so strong was the tendency to stress the communality of the liturgical celebration and to regard therefore the face-to-face position of priest and people as absolutely necessary.

More recently the atmosphere has become more relaxed so that it is possible to raise the kind of questions asked by Jungmann, Bouyer, and Gamber without at once being suspected of anti-conciliar sentiments. Historical research has made the controversy less partisan, and among the faithful there is an increasing sense of the problems inherent in an arrangement that hardly shows the liturgy to be open to the things that are above and to the world to come. In this situation, Lang's delightfully objective and wholly unpolemical book is a valuable guide. Without claiming to offer major new insights, he carefully presents the results of recent research and provides the material necessary for making an

informed judgment. The book is especially valuable in show-
ing the contribution made by the Church of England to this
question and in giving, also, due consideration to the part
played by the Oxford Movement in the nineteenth century
(in which the conversion of John Henry Newman ma-
tured). It is from such historical evidence that the author
elicits the theological answers that he proposes, and I hope
that the book, the work of a young scholar, will help the
struggle—necessary in every generation—for the right understanding and worthy celebration of the sacred liturgy. I
wish the book a wide and attentive readership.

Joseph Cardinal Ratzinger
Rome, Laetare Sunday 2003

ACKNOWLEDGMENTS

I am happy to acknowledge my debt to all those who contributed in many ways to the completion of this study. Thanks are due especially to Professors Sible de Blaauw, Peter Bruns, Stefan Heid, Bertram Stubenrauch, and Martin Wallraff, as well as to the Reverend Charles Scott Gibson, for their encouragement and criticism. I am most grateful to the Reverend Rupert McHardy, Richard and Elisabeth Dobbins for their invaluable help with translating my work from German into English, as well as to George McHardy and the Reverend van den Bergh for their careful proofreading of the manuscript. The illustrations are reproduced with the permission of Buch-Kunstverlag Ettal, Yale University Art Gallery, Librairie Orientaliste Paul Geuthner, Sible de Blaauw, and Institut d'Études Augustiniennes.

INTRODUCTION

The position of the altar and the direction taken by priest and people in liturgical worship have again become matters for theological debate. This seems a good occasion to publish a revised and substantially extended version of my essay 'Conversi ad Dominum: Zu Gebetsostung, Stellung des Liturgen am Altar und Kirchenbau'.[1] The intellectual and spiritual climate appears favourable to a recovery of the sacred direction in Christianity; this is clearly shown by recent studies on the subject which have been received with considerable attention among liturgical scholars.[2] As a preliminary conclusion of this discussion, it can be said that what is at issue is not so much the celebration of Mass 'facing the people' as the orientation of liturgical prayer.

In his review of my earlier study, Angelus Häußling found fault with my interpretation of the historical and theological material, which he criticises for drawing predictable conclusions.[3] I certainly aim at building a case on my reading of the sources, but this does not exonerate anyone who disagrees

[1] U. M. Lang, 'Conversi ad Dominum: Zu Gebetsostung, Stellung des Liturgen am Altar und Kirchenbau', *FKTh* 16 (2000): 81–123.

[2] See especially the monographs of S. de Blaauw (*Met het oog op het licht: Een vergeten principe in de oriëntatie van het vroegchristelijk kerkgebouw*, Nijmeegse Kunsthistorische Cahiers 2 [Nijmegen: Nijmegen University Press, 2000]) and M. Wallraff (*Christus verus sol: Sonnenverehrung und Christentum in der Spätantike*, JAC.E 32 [Münster: Aschendorff, 2001], 60–88).

[3] Cf. A. A. Häußling, review of U. M. Lang, 'Conversi ad Dominum: Zu Gebetsostung, Stellung des Liturgen am Altar und Kirchenbau' (*FKTh* 16 [2000]: 81–123), *ALW* 42 (2000): 156.

with me from evaluating my arguments. In the second, theological, part of my work I attempted to show the enduring significance of the common direction of liturgical prayer in the modern world. Häußling's chief objection is this:

> Against the intention of the Council, the author does not consider the most important argument in favour of the altered direction of the celebrant. The Council wanted to bring home the Paschal Mystery as the central event of salvation history (which is still present!). This means that the Lord, freed from death and exalted, lives in the middle of the Church, that is to say, in the middle of every praying community. Thus there can be no question that, in an age when man has made himself the centre of his own consciousness, when the greatness and the risks of human society shape our experience, the gathering of the faithful around the altar is felt to be more appropriate than the turning towards the east. The latter is often perceived as merely artificial, though 'objectively speaking', no less 'right'.[4]

In response to this criticism, I should like to note first that Häußling's reference to the 'intention of the Council' does not hold good. The importance of the Paschal Mystery for the life of the Church is beyond doubt, but the Council's emphasis on this central event of salvation history and its presence in the Church by no means requires that the priest face the people at Mass and thus suggest a gathering around the altar. Such an arrangement cannot account for the transcendent dynamism of the Paschal Mystery. Häußling then points to the prevalent anthropocentrism of our age; turning to the Lord is precisely a wholesome corrective to this mentality, since it can have a liberating effect and guide us to the fullness of the Divine Life. In this sense, Cardinal Ratzinger underlines the 'Exodus char-

---

[4] Translating ibid., 157.

acter' of the liturgy.[5] Reinhard Meßner refers to the 'eminently eschatological meaning' of orientation at prayer; it directs Christian existence towards Christ coming in glory. Meßner adds that the almost total loss of this liturgical tradition in the Roman Catholic Church of today indicates an eschatological deficit.[6] A similar note is struck by Andreas Heinz:

> The direction of prayer should point towards the transcendent addressee of prayer. Hence the question of the focal point of the presidential prayer needs to be considered seriously.... If the common direction of presider and congregation, in turning at prayer towards Christ, who has been exalted and is to come again, disappeared completely, it would be a regrettable spiritual loss.[7]

In two review articles, Albert Gerhards provides a fair and useful summary of recent contributions to the contentious discussion about *versus orientem* and *versus populum*.[8] He states, frankly:

> The Liturgical Movement certainly had a Trinitarian deficit in its Christocentrism, and this may have had an effect on

[5] Cf. J. Ratzinger, *The Spirit of the Liturgy*, trans. J. Saward (San Francisco: Ignatius Press, 2000), 12–23.

[6] Cf. R. Meßner, *Einführung in die Liturgiewissenschaft*, UTB 2173 (Paderborn: Schöningh, 2001).

[7] Translating A. Heinz, 'Ars celebrandi: Überlegungen zur Kunst, die Liturgie der Kirche zu feiern', *Questions Liturgiques* 83 (2002): 125.

[8] A. Gerhards, '"Blickt nach Osten!" Die Ausrichtung von Priester und Gemeinde bei der Eucharistie—eine kritische Reflexion nachkonziliarer Liturgiereform vor dem Hintergrund der Geschichte des Kirchenbaus', in *Liturgia et Unitas: Liturgiewissenschaftliche und ökumenische Studien zur Eucharistie und zum gottesdienstlichen Leben in der Schweiz: Études liturgiques et oecuméniques sur l'Eucharistie et la vie liturgique en Suisse: In honorem Bruno Bürki*, ed. M. Klöckener and A. Join-Lambert (Fribourg: Univ.-Verl., and Geneva: Labor et Fides, 2001), 197–217; and 'Versus orientem—versus populum: Zum gegenwärtigen Diskussionsstand einer alten Streitfrage', *ThRv* 98 (2002): 15–22.

the liturgy of the Second Vatican Council. Both Ratzinger and Lang rightly reclaim this dimension.[9]

It would seem questionable, to say the least, whether the present shape of Catholic worship can simply be identified as the 'liturgy of the Second Vatican Council'. Be that as it may, Gerhards concedes that there are deficiencies in contemporary liturgical practice:

> Authors like Ratzinger and Lang have shown the problems inherent in the constant face-to-face position [of priest and people at Mass], which is also called into question by the experience of community practice.[10]

Gerhards also observes that present liturgical scholarship is quite favourable to recovering the category of sacrifice. As he rightly stresses, the sacrificial understanding of the Eucharist should not be played off against its character as a sacred banquet.[11] It would seem obvious to me that there is a connection between sacrifice and direction of prayer,[12] but, to establish this point, further in-depth study will be needed. An interesting field for research appears to be Syrian Christianity, where both literary and archaeological evidence for liturgical orientation is clearest, while at the same time the sacrificial aspect of the Eucharist is fully developed by theologians such as Theodore of Mopsuestia and Narsai.

[9] Translating Gerhards, 'Versus orientem', 20.

[10] Translating Gerhards, '"Blickt nach Osten!"', 208. For a similar criticism, see L. van Tongeren, 'Vers une utilisation dynamique et flexible de l'espace: Une réflexion renouvelée sur le réaménagement d'églises', *Questions Liturgiques* 83 (2002): 165: 'Cela favorise une consommation passive plutôt qu'une participation active.... Le chœur adresse la louange de Dieu à l'assemblée, et ... le président n'adresse pas sa prière à Dieu mais à l'assemblée; il ne précède pas l'assemblée dans la prière mais adresse une prière en présence de la communauté.'

[11] Cf. Gerhards, '"Blickt nach Osten!"', 210.

[12] *Pace* Häußling, review of Lang, 157.

I have suggested a combination between priest and people facing each other for the Introductory Rites, the Liturgy of the Word, parts of the Communion Rite, and the Concluding Rite, and a common direction of prayer for the Liturgy of the Eucharist in the strict sense, especially the canon. This proposal has been criticised from different points of view. Rudolf Kaschewsky highlights the 'latreutic' element for the proclamation of the Word and holds that it is appropriate and necessary for the Scriptural readings too that priest and people should face the same way.[13] From quite a different perspective Gerhards argues that my proposal puts the axiom of common direction itself into question.[14]

The proclamation of the Word of God certainly has a latreutic element in it, especially when it is done in a solemn way (candles, incense, procession with the Gospel book, and singing of the pericope). In my opinion neither objection takes into account the different aspects of the Liturgy of the Word and the Liturgy of the Eucharist. The 'katabatic' aspect comes to the fore when the congregation listens to the Word of God being proclaimed and interpreted; the 'anabatic' aspect comes to the fore during the eucharistic liturgy (excepting the distribution of Holy Communion), when the congregation under the leadership of the priest is before the Lord to offer the sacrifice of Christ and of the Church.[15]

---

[13] R. Kaschewsky, 'Eine wichtige Veröffentlichung zur Zelebration *versus populum*', *UVK* 30 (2000): 311.

[14] Gerhards, 'Versus orientem', 18.

[15] In his very personal attack on Cardinal Ratzinger's book *The Spirit of the Liturgy*, Pierre-Marie Gy also talks about the direction of liturgical prayer. His comments, however, reflect neither the current state of historical research nor the present theological debate: Gy, '*L'Esprit de la liturgie* du Cardinal Ratzinger est-il fidèle au Concile, ou en réaction contre?' *La Maison-Dieu* 229 (2002): 173–75. See now the response of Ratzinger: '*L'Esprit de la liturgie* ou la fidelité au Concile: Réponse au Père Gy', *La Maison-Dieu* 230 (2002): 114–20.

The Reform of the Liturgy and the Position of the Celebrant at the Altar

The reform of the Roman Rite of Mass that was carried out after the Second Vatican Council has significantly altered the shape of Catholic worship. One of the most evident changes was the construction of freestanding altars. The *versus populum* celebration was adopted throughout the Latin Church, and, with few exceptions, it has become the prevailing practice during Mass for the celebrant to stand behind the altar facing the congregation. This uniformity has led to the widespread misunderstanding that the priest's 'turning his back on the people' is characteristic of the rite of Mass according to the Missal of Pope Saint Pius V whereas the priest's 'turning towards the people' belongs to the *Novus Ordo* Mass of Pope Paul VI. It is also widely assumed by the general public that the celebration of Mass 'facing the people' is required, indeed even imposed, by the liturgical reform that was inaugurated by Vatican II.

However, the relevant conciliar and post-conciliar documents present quite a different picture. The Council's Constitution on the Sacred Liturgy, *Sacrosanctum Concilium*, speaks neither of a celebration *versus populum* nor of the setting up of new altars. In view of this fact it is all the more astonishing how rapidly *'versus populum* altars' appeared in Catholic churches all over the world.[1] The instruction *Inter Oecumenici*, prepared by the *Consilium* for the carrying out of the Constitution on the Sacred Liturgy and issued on 26 September 1964, has a chapter on the designing of new churches and altars that includes the following paragraph:

> Praestat ut altare maius exstruatur a pariete seiunctum, ut facile circumiri et in eo celebratio versus populum peragi possit. [It is better for the main altar to be constructed away from the wall so that one can easily walk around the altar and celebrate facing the people.][2]

It is said to be desirable to set up the main altar separate from the back wall, so that the priest can walk around it easily and a celebration facing the people is *possible*. Josef Andreas Jungmann asks us to consider this:

> It is only the possibility that is emphasised. And this [separation of the altar from the wall] is not even prescribed, but is only recommended, as one will see if one looks at the Latin text of the directive.... In the new instruction the general permission of such an altar layout is stressed only with regard to possible obstacles or local restrictions.[3]

In a letter addressed to the heads of bishops' conferences, dated 25 January 1966, Cardinal Giacomo Lercaro, the pres-

[1] J. A. Jungmann, 'Der neue Altar', *Der Seelsorger* 37 (1967): 375.

[2] Sacra Congregatio Rituum, *Instructio ad exsecutionem Constitutionis de sacra Liturgia recte ordinandam 'Inter Oecumenici', AAS* 56 (1964): 898, no. 91. This translation is more literal than the one found in *Documents on the Liturgy, 1963–1979: Conciliar, Papal, and Curial Texts* (Collegeville, Minn.: Liturgical Press, 1982), 108, no. 383.

[3] Translating Jungmann, 'Der neue Altar', 375.

ident of the *Consilium*, states that regarding the renewal of altars 'prudence must be our guide'. He goes on to explain:

> Above all because for a living and participated liturgy, it is not indispensable that the altar should be *versus populum*: in the Mass, the entire liturgy of the word is celebrated at the chair, ambo or lectern, and, therefore, facing the assembly; as to the eucharistic liturgy, loudspeaker systems make participation feasible enough. Secondly, hard thought should be given to the artistic and architectural question, this element in many places being protected by rigorous civil laws.[4]

With reference to Cardinal Lercaro's exhortation to prudence, Jungmann warns us not to make the option granted by the instruction into 'an absolute demand, and eventually a fashion, to which one succumbs without thinking'.[5]

Inter Oecumenici permits the Mass facing the people, but it does not prescribe it. As Louis Bouyer emphasised in 1967, that document does not at all suggest that Mass facing the people is always the preferable form of eucharistic celebration.[6] The rubrics of the renewed *Missale Romanum* of Pope Paul VI presuppose a common direction of priest and

[4] G. Lercaro, 'L'Heureux Développement', *Not* 2 (1966): 160; English translation: *Documents on the Liturgy*, 122, no. 428.

[5] Translating Jungmann, 'Der neue Altar', 380; see also C. Napier, 'The Altar in the Contemporary Church', *CleR* 57 (1972): 624. A. Lorenzer, ' "Sacrosanctum Concilium": Der Anfang der "Buchhalterei": Betrachtungen aus psychoanalytisch-kulturkritischer Sicht', in *Gottesdienst–Kirche–Gesellschaft: Interdisziplinäre und ökumenische Standortbestimmungen nach 25 Jahren Liturgiereform*, ed. H. Becker, B. J. Hilberath, and U. Willers, PiLi 5 (St. Ottilien: EOS-Verlag, 1991), 158, argues that there is a significant difference between the conciliar documents and what came out of them. Whereas the texts carefully present a number of options, their implementation became an exercise in 'total deforestation'.

[6] L. Bouyer, *Liturgy and Architecture* (Notre Dame, Ind.: University of Notre Dame Press, 1967), 105–6.

people for the core of the eucharistic liturgy. This is indicated by the instruction that, at the *Orate, fratres*, the *Pax
Domini*, the *Ecce, Agnus Dei*, and the *Ritus conclusionis*, the
priest should turn towards the people.[7] This would seem to
imply that beforehand priest and people were facing the same
direction, that is, towards the altar. At the priest's communion the rubrics say '*ad altare versus*',[8] which would be re-
dundant if the celebrant stood behind the altar facing the
people anyway. This reading is confirmed by the directives
of the *General Instruction*, even if they are occasionally at vari-
ance with the *Ordo Missae*.[9] The third *Editio typica* of the
renewed *Missale Romanum*, approved by Pope John Paul II
on 10 April 2000 and published in spring 2002, retains these
rubrics.[10]

---

[7] *Missale Romanum ex decreto Sacrosancti Oecumenici Concilii Vaticani II instauratum auctoritate Pauli PP. VI promulgatum*, editio typica (Vatican City: Typis Polyglottis Vaticanis, 1970), *Ordo Missae cum populo*, 391, no. 25 (*versus ad populum*),
473, no. 128 (*ad populum conversus*), 474, no. 133 (*ad populum versus*), and 475,
no. 142 (*versus ad populum*).

[8] Ibid., 474, no. 134.

[9] Ibid., *Institutio Generalis*, nos. 107, 115, 116, 122, as well as 198 and 199 for
concelebrated Masses. Cf. O. Nußbaum, 'Die Zelebration versus populum
und der Opfercharakter der Messe', *ZKTh* 93 (1971): 149–50, who points out
how little the liturgical reform wished to make *versus populum* celebration into
the exclusive norm. This, he thinks, is clearly demonstrated by the fact that in
the revision of the *Ritus servandus in celebratione Missae*, and subsequently also
in the 1965 and 1967 versions of the *Ordo Missae*, the celebrant was still explicitly instructed to turn towards the people when addressing them directly,
as for example in the liturgical greeting. The *Novus Ordo Missae* also keeps to
this practice within the eucharistic liturgy. Nußbaum was certainly an advocate of *versus populum* celebration, and yet he concedes that, in the reform of
the liturgy, this was not the preferred option let alone the only legitimate way
of celebrating Mass.

[10] *Missale Romanum ex decreto Sacrosancti Oecumenici Concilii Vaticani II instauratum auctoritate Pauli PP. VI promulgatum Ioannis Pauli PP. II cura recognitum*,
editio typica tertia (Vatican City: Typis Vaticanis, 2002), *Ordo Missae*, 515, no. 28;
600, no. 127; 601, nos. 132–33; 603, no. 141.

This interpretation of the official documents has been endorsed by the Roman Congregation for Divine Worship. An editorial in its official publication, *Notitiae*, states that the arrangement of an altar that permits a celebration facing the people is not a question upon which the liturgy stands or falls ('quaestio stantis vel cadentis liturgiae'). Furthermore, the article suggests that, in this matter as in many others, Cardinal Lercaro's call for prudence was hardly heard in the post-conciliar euphoria. The editorial observes that changing the orientation of the altar and using the vernacular could become an easy substitute for entering into the theological and spiritual dimensions of the liturgy, for studying its history and for taking into account the pastoral consequences of the reform.[11]

The revised *General Instruction of the Roman Missal*, which was published for study purposes in the spring of 2000, has a paragraph bearing on the altar question:

> Altare exstruatur a pariete seiunctum, ut facile circumiri et in eo celebratio versus populum peragi possit, quod expedit ubicumque possibile sit. [Let the main altar be constructed separate from the wall so that one can easily walk around the altar and celebrate facing the people—which is desirable wherever possible.][12]

The subtle wording of this paragraph (*possit—possibile*) clearly indicates that the position of the celebrant priest facing the people is not made compulsory. The instruction merely allows for both forms of celebration. At any rate, the added phrase 'which is desirable wherever (or whenever) possible

---

[11] Congregatio de Cultu Divino et Disciplina Sacramentorum, 'Editoriale: Pregare "ad orientem versus"', *Not* 29 (1993): 247.

[12] *Missale Romanum* (2002), *Institutio Generalis*, no. 299.

(quod expedit ubicumque possibile sit)' refers to the provision for a freestanding altar and not to the desirability of celebration towards the people.[13] Nonetheless various news reports about the revised *General Instruction* seemed to suggest that the position of the celebrant *versus orientem* or *versus absidem* was declared undesirable, if not prohibited. This interpretation however has been rejected by the Congregation for Divine Worship in a response to a question submitted by Cardinal Christoph Schönborn, Archbishop of Vienna. The response is dated 25 September 2000 and signed by Cardinal Jorge Arturo Medina Estévez, then Prefect of the Congregation, and Archbishop Francesco Pio Tamburrino, its Secretary:

> In the first place, it is to be borne in mind that the word *expedit* does not constitute an obligation, but a suggestion that refers to the construction of the altar *a pariete seiunctum* (detached from the wall) and to the celebration *versus populum* (towards the people). The clause *ubi* [*sic*] *possibile sit* (where it is possible) refers to different elements, as, for example, the topography of the place, the availability of space, the artistic value of the existing altar, the sensibility of the people participating in the celebrations in a particular church, etc. It reaffirms that the position towards the assembly seems more convenient inasmuch as it makes communication easier (cf. the editorial in *Notitiae* 29 [1993] 245–49), without excluding, however, the other possibility.
>
> However, whatever may be the position of the celebrating priest, it is clear that the eucharistic sacrifice is offered to the one and triune God and that the principal, eternal, and high priest is Jesus Christ, who acts through the ministry of

---

[13] The text is carefully scrutinised by C. M. Cullen and J. W. Koterski, 'The New IGMR and Mass *versus Populum*', *Homiletic and Pastoral Review*, June 2001, 51–54.

the priest who visibly presides as his instrument. The liturgical assembly participates in the celebration in virtue of the common priesthood of the faithful which requires the ministry of the ordained priest to be exercised in the eucharistic synaxis. The physical position, especially with respect to the communication among the various members of the assembly, must be distinguished from the interior spiritual orientation of all. It would be a grave error to imagine that the principal orientation of the sacrificial action is towards the community. If the priest celebrates *versus populum*, which is legitimate and often advisable, his spiritual attitude ought always to be *versus Deum per Iesum Christum* (towards God through Jesus Christ), as representative of the entire Church. The Church as well, which takes concrete form in the assembly which participates, is entirely turned *versus Deum* (towards God) as its first spiritual movement.[14]

Obviously, the relevant paragraph of the *General Instruction* must be read in light of this clarification.[15]

Already in the sixties, theologians of international renown criticised the sweeping triumph of the celebration *versus populum*. In addition to Jungmann and Bouyer, Joseph Ratzinger, then professor of theology at Tübingen and *peritus* at the Council, delivered a lecture at the *Katholikentag* of 1966 in Bamberg that was received with much attention. His observations have lost nothing of their relevance:

[14] Congregatio de Cultu Divino et Disciplina Sacramentorum, 'Responsa ad quaestiones de nova *Institutione Generali Missalis Romani*', *CCCIC* 32 (2000): 171–72. Surprisingly, it has been published, not in *Notitiae*, but in *Communicationes*, the official publication of the Pontifical Council for the Interpretation of Legal Texts. The English translation is taken from *Adoremus Bulletin Online Edition*, vol. 6, no. 9 (December 2000–January 2001), ⟨http://www. adoremus.org/12-0101cdw-adorient.html⟩ (accessed 5 January 2004).

[15] Cf. The comments of J. Nebel, 'Die *editio typica tertia* des *Missale Romanum*: Eine Untersuchung über die Veränderungen', *Ecclesia Orans* 19 (2002): 278, n. 72.

We can no longer deny that exaggerations and aberrations have crept in which are both annoying and unbecoming. Must every Mass, for instance, be celebrated facing the people? Is it so absolutely important to be able to look the priest in the face, or might it not be often very salutary to reflect that he also is a Christian and that he has every reason to turn to God with all his fellow-Christians of the congregation and to say together with them 'Our Father'?[16]

The German liturgist Balthasar Fischer concedes that the turning of the celebrant towards the people for the entire celebration of the Mass was never officially introduced or prescribed by the new liturgical legislation. In post-conciliar documents it was merely declared possible. In view of this, however, the fact that the celebration *versus populum* has become the dominant practice of the Latin Church shows the astounding extent to which 'the active role of the people in the celebration of the Eucharist' has been realised; for Fischer this is indeed the fundamental issue of the liturgical reform after Vatican II.[17]

Two main arguments in favour of the celebrant's position facing the people during the Eucharist are usually presented. First, it is claimed that this was the practice of the early Church that should be the norm for our age. Second, it is maintained that the 'active participation' of the faithful, a principle that was introduced by Pope Saint Pius X and is central to *Sacrosanctum Concilium*, demanded the celebration towards the people.[18] The aim of this study will be to counter these

[16] J. Ratzinger, 'Catholicism after the Council', trans. P. Russell, *The Furrow* 18 (1967): 11–12.

[17] B. Fischer, 'Die Grundaussagen der Liturgie-Konstitution und ihre Rezeption in fünfundzwanzig Jahren', in Becker, Hilberath, and Willers, *Gottesdienst–Kirche–Gesellschaft*, 422–23.

[18] See, for instance, O. Nußbaum, *Der Standort des Liturgen am christlichen Altar vor dem Jahre 1000: Eine archäologische und liturgiegeschichtliche Untersuchung,*

arguments in a twofold way. First, an examination of the historical evidence will show that the orientation of priest and people in the liturgy of the Eucharist is well-attested in the early Church and was, in fact, the general custom. It will be evident that the common direction of liturgical prayer has been a consistent tradition in both the East and the West. Second, I should like to argue, relying on the thought of contemporary theologians, that the permanent face-to-face position of priest and people is not beneficial for a real participation of the faithful in the liturgy, as envisaged by Vatican II. Recent critical reflection on *participatio actuosa* has revealed the need for a theological reappraisal and deepening of this important principle. Cardinal Ratzinger draws a useful distinction between participation in the Liturgy of the Word, which includes external actions, especially reading and singing, and participation in the Liturgy of the Eucharist, where external actions are quite secondary. He writes:

> *Doing* really must stop when we come to the heart of the matter: the *oratio*. It must be plainly evident that the *oratio* is the heart of the matter, but that it is important precisely because it provides a space for the *actio* of God. Anyone who grasps this will easily see that it is not now a matter of looking at or toward the priest, but of looking together toward the Lord and going out to meet him.[19]

Theoph 18 (Bonn: Hanstein, 1965), 1:22, and B. Neunheuser, 'Eucharistiefeier am Altare *versus populum*: Geschichte und Problematik', in *Florentissima proles Ecclesiae: Miscellanea hagiographica, historica et liturgica Reginaldo Grégoire O.S.B. XII lustra complenti oblata*, ed. D. Gobbi (Trento: Civis, 1996), 442–43.

[19] J. Ratzinger, *The Spirit of the Liturgy*, trans. J. Saward (San Francisco: Ignatius Press, 2000), 174, cf. 171–77. See also the critical remarks of M. Kunzler, 'La liturgia all'inizio del Terzo Millennio', in *Il Concilio Vaticano II: Recezione e attualità alla luce del Giubileo*, ed. R. Fisichella (Milan: San Paolo, 2000), 217–24, and D. Torevell, *Losing the Sacred: Ritual, Modernity and Liturgical Reform* (Edinburgh: T and T Clark, 2000).

The statement of the Congregation for Divine Worship already quoted shows that speaking of 'celebrating towards the people' indicates merely the position of the priest vis-à-vis the congregation at certain parts of the liturgy but does not refer to a theological concept.[20] The expression *versus (ad) populum* seems to have been used for the first time by the papal master of ceremonies, Johannes Burckard, in his *Ordo Missae* of 1502[21] and was taken up in the *Ritus servandus in celebratione Missae* of the *Missale Romanum* that Pope Saint Pius V issued in 1570. The *Ritus servandus* deals with the case where the altar is directed to the east and, at the same time, towards the people (*altare sit ad orientem, versus populum*). This is indeed the state of affairs in the major Roman basilicas with the entrance facing east and the apse facing west. Here *versus populum* is to be looked upon merely as an explanatory appositive, namely in view of the immediately following directive that in this case at the *Pax Domini* the celebrant does not need to turn around (*non vertit humeros ad altare*), since he already stands *ad populum* anyway.[22] It is in this topographical sense that the similar passages in Amalarius (ca. 830)[23] and Durandus (to-

[20] Congregatio de Cultu Divino et Disciplina Sacramentorum, 'Editoriale', 249.

[21] Johannes Burckard, *Ordo Missae Ioannis Burckardi*, ed. J. W. Legg, *Tracts on the Mass*, HBS 27 (London: Harrison, 1904), 142; cf. Nußbaum, 'Die Zelebration versus populum', 160–61.

[22] *Missale Romanum ex decreto Sacrosancti Concilii Tridentini restitutum Pii V Pont. Max. iussu editum, Ritus servandus in celebratione Missae*, V, 3. The 1570 *editio princeps* of this Missal is now accessible in a study edition: M. Sodi and A. M. Triacca, eds., *Missale Romanum: Editio Princeps (1570)*, Monumenta Liturgica Concilii Tridentini 2 (Vatican City: Libreria Editrice Vaticana, 1998).

[23] Amalarius uses the expressions *ad orientem* and *ad populum* for explaining that the celebrant stands in front of the altar facing east and turns around for the liturgical greeting: *Liber officialis* III, 9, ed. J. M. Hanssens, Studi e Testi, 139, 1:288–90. On Amalarius, see now W. Steck, *Der Liturgiker Amalarius: Eine*

wards the end of the thirteenth century)[24] are also to be understood.

When these texts use the phrase *versus populum*, they do not necessarily mean a visual connection between the people and the sacred action at the altar. It is by no means suggested here that nothing should limit, let alone block, the faithful's view of the ritual acts of the celebrant. Such an interpretation would have seemed alien to the understanding of the liturgy that was common from Christian antiquity until well into the Middle Ages and is still found in the Eastern Churches. Thus it is hardly surprising to find that even with altars *versus populum* the sight was significantly restricted, for example, by curtains that were closed during certain parts of the liturgy or already by the architectural layout of the church.[25]

The guiding points of the Congregation for Divine Worship make clear that the expression *versus populum* does not convey the theological dimension of the eucharistic liturgy. Each Eucharist is offered for the praise and glory of God's name, for the benefit of us and of the holy Church as a whole ('ad laudem et gloriam nominis Dei, ad utilitatem quoque nostram, totiusque Ecclesiae suae sanctae'). Theologically, the Mass as a whole, the Liturgy of the Word and the Liturgy of the Eucharist, is directed at the same time

---

quellenkritische Untersuchung zu Leben und Werk eines Theologen der Karolingerzeit, MThS.H 35 (Munich: St. Ottilien: EOS-Verlag, 2000).

[24] 'In ecclesiis vero ostia ab oriente habentibus, ut Rome, nulla est in salutatione necessaria conversio, quia sacerdos in illis celebrans semper ad populum stat conversus' (Durandus, *Rationale divinorum officiorum* V, II, 57: CChr.CM 140A, 42–43).

[25] Nußbaum, *Der Standort des Liturgen,* 1:418–19, and J. A. Jungmann, review of O. Nußbaum, *Der Standort des Liturgen am christlichen Altar vor dem Jahre 1000,* ZKTh 88 (1966): 447.

towards God and towards the people. In the form of the celebration one must avoid a confusion of theology and topography, especially when the priest stands at the altar. The priest speaks to the people only during the dialogues at the altar. Everything else is prayer to the Father through Christ in the Holy Spirit. Evidently, it is most desirable that this theology should be expressed in the visible shape of the liturgy.[26]

Cardinal Ratzinger is equally emphatic that the celebration of the Eucharist, just as Christian prayer in general, has a trinitarian direction and discusses the question of how this can be communicated most fittingly in liturgical gesture. When we speak to someone, we obviously face that person. Accordingly, the whole liturgical assembly, priest and people, should face the same way, turning towards God to whom prayers and offerings are addressed in this common act of trinitarian worship. Ratzinger rightly protests against the mistaken idea that in this case the celebrating priest is facing 'towards the altar', 'towards the tabernacle', or even 'towards the wall'.[27] The catchphrase often heard nowadays that the priest is 'turning his back on the people' is a classic example of confounding theology and topography, for the crucial point is that the Mass is a common act of worship where priest and people together, representing the pilgrim Church, reach out for the transcendent God.

Reinhard Meßner notes that what is at issue is not the *celebratio versus populum*, but the direction of liturgical prayer that has been known in the Christian tradition as 'facing

---

[26] Congregatio de Cultu Divino et Disciplina Sacramentorum, 'Editoriale', 249.

[27] J. Ratzinger, *The Feast of Faith: Approaches to a Theology of the Liturgy*, trans. G. Harrison (San Francisco: Ignatius Press, 1986), 139–43.

east'.[28] My claim is that the intrinsic sense of facing east in the Eucharist is the common direction of priest and people oriented towards the triune God. The following chapters on the historical and theological dimensions of this traditional liturgical practice are meant to show that its recovery is indispensable for the welfare of the Church today.

[28] R. Meßner, 'Probleme des eucharistischen Hochgebets', in *Bewahren und Erneuern: Studien zur Meßliturgie: Festschrift für Hans Bernhard Meyer SJ zum 70. Geburtstag*, ed. R. Meßner, E. Nagel, and R. Pacik, IThS 42 (Innsbruck and Vienna: Tyrolia, 1995), 201, n. 99; likewise M. Wallraff, *Christus verus sol: Sonnenverehrung und Christentum in der Spätantike*, JAC.E 32 (Münster: Aschendorff, 2001), 72, n. 53.

II

Direction of Prayer, Liturgy, and Church Architecture in the Early Church

1. Facing East: The Christian Direction of Prayer

In most major religions, the position taken in prayer and the layout of holy places are determined by a 'sacred direction'. For the history of religions the term 'sacred direction' is more appropriate than 'orientation', since the latter specifically indicates a turning towards the east. Franz Joseph Dölger shows in his seminal study on orientation in prayer and liturgy[1] that turning towards the east in prayer was a general custom in the sun-worship of the ancient world from the Mediterranean to India.[2] A variant of this principle can be found in Manicheism. Saint Augustine, a 'hearer' of this religion for some years before his conversion, reports that the

---

[1] F. J. Dölger, *Sol salutis: Gebet und Gesang im christlichen Altertum: Mit besonderer Rücksicht auf die Ostung in Gebet und Liturgie*, 2d ed., LF 4/5 (Münster: Aschendorff, 1925); see now also A. Podossinov, 'Himmelsrichtung (kultische)', *RAC* 15 (1991): 233–86, and M. Wallraff, *Christus verus sol: Sonnenverehrung und Christentum in der Spätantike*, JAC.E 32 (Münster: Aschendorff, 2001), 60–88.

[2] Dölger, *Sol salutis*, 20–38. On the difficult question of sun-worship and the cult of Yahweh in ancient Israel, see the study of J. G. Taylor, *Yahweh and the Sun: Biblical and Archaeological Evidence for Sun Worship in Ancient Israel*, JSOT, supplement 111 (Sheffield: JSOT Press, 1993), with a comprehensive bibliography.

Manicheans, in their prayers, used to follow the course of the sun and turn towards its actual position. This practice was attacked by Christians as contrary to the faith.[3] Turning towards the rising sun for prayer was customary among the Greeks, for example in the Neoplatonic theurgy of Proclus. Such orientation was also observed in Roman religion. In fact, facing east became detached from the cult of the sun and independent of the time of prayer. The eastern sky was regarded as the home of the gods and thus as a symbol of fortune.[4]

The early Christians defined their identity through a critical discernment of their pagan surroundings in the Roman Empire. If we attempt to understand the Christian idea of sacred direction, it is not sufficient to look at the context of pagan thought and practice;[5] rather, we must consider the process by which Christianity became separate from Judaism. Jews in the Diaspora prayed towards Jerusalem, or, more precisely, towards the presence of the transcendent God (*shekinah*) in the Holy of Holies of the Temple. For instance, Daniel in Babylon 'went to his house where he had windows in his upper chamber open to Jerusalem; and he got down upon his knees three times a day and prayed and gave thanks before his God, as he had done previously' (Dan 6:10).[6] Even

---

[3] Augustine, *C. Fortunatum* 3: CSEL 25, 84–85; *C. Faustum* XIV, 11: CSEL 25, 411–12, and XX, 5: 540.

[4] Cf. Dölger, *Sol salutis*, 38–60.

[5] W. Burkert, *Klassisches Altertum und antikes Christentum: Probleme einer übergreifenden Religionswissenschaft*, Hans-Lietzmann-Vorlesungen 1 (Berlin: Walter de Gruyter, 1996), 43, emphasises the originality of Judaism and Christianity in the context of late antiquity. On this point, see also C. Vogel, 'La Croix eschatologique', in A. M. Dubarle et al., *Noël, Épiphanie, retour du Christ*, Lex orandi 40 (Paris: Éditions du Cerf, 1967), 85–108.

[6] Cf. 1 Kings 8:38, 44, 48, and the corresponding instructions in the Mishnah, *Berakhot* 4, 5, and the Tosefta, *Berakhot* 3, 15–16.

after the destruction of the Temple, the prevailing custom of turning towards Jerusalem for prayer was kept in the liturgy of the synagogue. Thus Jews have expressed their eschatological hope for the coming of the Messiah, the rebuilding of the Temple, and the gathering of God's people from the Diaspora. The direction of prayer was thus inseparably bound up with the messianic expectation of Israel.[7]

Georg Kretschmar sees a connection between the development of the eastward direction of prayer among Christians and a local tradition of the primitive Church in Jerusalem. Interpreting some Old Testament prophecies (Ezek 11:23, 43:1–2, 44:1–2, and Zech 14:4), the earliest Christians expected the Second Coming of the Lord to be on the Mount of Olives, which was revered as the place of his Ascension (Acts 1:9–12). On the eve of the Passover, at any rate, the Christians of Jerusalem prayed turning towards the Mount of Olives. Given the topography of the city, this meant that they were facing east. After the devastating events of A.D. 70, the expectation of the Parousia became detached from the Mount of Olives, while the eastward direction of prayer was retained and developed into a general principle.[8] Stefan Heid objects to Kretschmar's suggestion because the sources for a local tradition that the Second Coming was expected on the Mount of Olives do not reach back before A.D. 70. Hence it is uncertain whether it was customary for the primitive Christian community at this early date to pray towards the Mount of Olives. Furthermore, owing to the topography of Jerusalem, Jews, when not within the Temple precincts, would

---

[7] Cf. E. Peterson, *Frühkirche, Judentum und Gnosis: Studien und Untersuchungen* (Freiburg: Herder, 1959), 1–4, and L. Bouyer, *Liturgy and Architecture* (Notre Dame, Ind.: University of Notre Dame Press, 1967), 17–20.

[8] G. Kretschmar, 'Festkalender und Memorialstätten Jerusalems in altkirchlicher Zeit', *ZDPV* 87 (1971): 201–5.

also have turned towards the east or northeast, that is to say, towards the Holy of Holies—and so in the direction of the Mount of Olives.[9]

Be this as it may, it would seem obvious that, because of its messianic connotation, the direction of prayer was at the heart of the controversies that finally led to the separation of Christianity from Judaism. However, this process cannot be understood merely as a demarcation on the part of the early Church. It was not simply the case that the early Christians replaced the Jewish practice of turning towards Jerusalem with the practice of turning towards the east in prayer. Rather, the situation seems not to have been as clear-cut as used to be thought. Prayer facing east was also known to the Jewish tradition (cf. Wis 16:28),[10] both among the Essenes and in the rabbinical Judaism of the first centuries A.D. There is archaeological evidence of synagogues from the second to the fourth century with the doors on the eastern side of the building. The Tosefta attests that after the sack of Jerusalem in A.D. 70 certain parts of Judaism attempted to copy the orientation of the Temple, whose Holy of Holies opened towards the east. Later this imitation of the Temple layout, which must have spread to some extent, was forbidden by a Palestinian rabbi, as recorded in the Babylonian Talmud.[11] The community in a synagogue with the entrance facing east turned presumably towards the doors, not towards the west wall.[12] This would correspond to the basic sense of

---

[9] S. Heid, *Kreuz—Jerusalem—Kosmos:Aspekte frühchristlicher Staurologie*, JAC.E 31 (Münster: Aschendorff, 2001), 150–59.

[10] For the interpretation of this passage in the Hellenistic-Jewish milieu of Alexandria, see Dölger, *Sol salutis*, 165–67.

[11] See Tosefta, *Megillah* 4[3], 22, and Babylonian Talmud, *Menahot* 109b.

[12] This point is not noticed by J. Wilkinson, 'Orientation, Jewish and Christian', *PEQ* 116 (1984): 16–30.

people in the ancient world that, if possible, one should say one's prayers towards the open sky. In a closed room one would turn to an open door or an open window. Many synagogues from the time after the destruction of the Temple are directed with their entrance towards Jerusalem, especially in Galilee.[13] With the development of a fixed shrine for the Torah on the wall opposite the entrance, a conflict seems to have arisen between the veneration of Holy Scripture and the turning towards the doors for prayer. Eventually, the idea gained acceptance that the wall with the Torah shrine, and no longer the entrance, indicated the 'sacred direction'.[14]

Martin Wallraff maintains that up to the second century, prayer towards the east was just as common in Judaism as prayer towards Jerusalem. He also argues that this was similar in early Christianity, as shown by the practice of the Elchasaites and the Ebionites. Epiphanius of Salamis reports that Elchasai, the leader of a Judaeo-Christian sect towards the end of the first century, forbade the eastward direction in prayer (which must already have been the custom among the Christians of Palestine and Syria) and prescribed the direction

---

[13] Cf. F. Landsberger, 'The Sacred Direction in Synagogue and Church', *HUCA* 28 (1957): 181–203; A. R. Seager, 'The Architecture of the Dura and Sardis Synagogues', in *The Dura-Europos Synagogue: A Re-evaluation (1932–1972)*, ed. J. Gutmann (Missoula, Mont.: University of Montana, 1973), 79–116, and 'Ancient Synagogue Architecture: An Overview', in *Ancient Synagogues: The State of Research*, ed. J. Gutmann, BJSt 22 (Chico, Calif.: Scholars Press, 1981), 39–47; and M. Wallraff, 'La preghiera verso l'oriente: Alle origini di un uso liturgico', in *La preghiera nel tardo antico: Dalle origini a Sant' Agostino: XXVII Incontro di studiosi dell' antichità cristiana, Roma, 7–9 maggio 1998*, SEAug 66 (Rome: Institutum Patristicum Augustinianum, 1999), 463–69. A trace of this practice may still be found in the custom where the congregation turns towards the door of the synagogue to greet the Sabbath, while the hymn *Lekha dodi* is chanted; see M. Wallraff, 'Die Ursprünge der christlichen Gebetsostung', *ZKG* 111 (2000): 179, n. 34.

[14] Landsberger, 'Sacred Direction', 181–93.

towards Jerusalem.[15] Wallraff considers the clear distinction suggested by Epiphanius between Judaism and Christianity to be an anachronism that does not do justice to the complex picture of the first century, when the primitive Church still shared in Jewish traditions. The formation of the specifically Christian (just as the specifically Jewish) direction of prayer came about, not through a unilateral separation of Christianity from Judaism, but rather through a process of mutual stimulus and disaffection.[16] Wallraff succeeds in demonstrating that the relationship between Judaism and Christianity in the first two centuries A.D. was more complex than is often assumed, in particular with regard to the direction of prayer: there were Jews who turned towards the east, and there were Christians who turned towards Jerusalem. Nonetheless it would seem, at least in my view, that facing east in prayer was a rather marginal tradition in Judaism and was eventually given up because it was perceived to be the specifically Christian direction of prayer.[17] True, the Christian idea of praying towards the east had a Jewish precedent. Inevitably, however, the connection between sacred direction and messianic expectation led to a conflict between Jews and Christians on that issue, according to the principle: *lex orandi—lex credendi*.[18]

---

[15] Epiphanius, *Panarion, haer.* 19, 3, 5–6: GCS Epiph. I, 220: cf. Dölger, *Sol salutis*, 194–98. About the Ebionites, see Irenaeus of Lyons, *Haer.* I, 26, 2: SC 264, 346: "Hierosolymam adorent quasi domus sit Dei."

[16] Wallraff, 'La preghiera verso l'oriente', 468.

[17] According to the Babylonian Talmud, blind Rabbi Shesheth (third or fourth century) instructed his servant that he could position him at prayer in any direction except east, since the followers of Jesus chose this one. Babylonian Talmud, *Baba Bathra* 2, 9–10 (25a); for the textual difficulty of this passage, see Wallraff, 'Die Ursprünge', 179, n. 36.

[18] Landsberger, 'Sacred Direction', 181: 'It is striking that the position taken in prayer and in the layout of sacred structures has not been left to chance but has been determined by the prevailing religious outlook.' For the Jewish direction of prayer, see also Podossinov, 'Himmelsrichtung (kultische)', 247–53.

There is no doubt that, from very early times, it was a matter of course for Christians all over the known world to turn in prayer towards the rising sun, that is to say, towards the geographical east.[19] In private and in liturgical prayer Christians turned, no longer towards the earthly Jerusalem, but towards the new, heavenly Jerusalem; they believed firmly that when the Lord came again in glory to judge the world, he would gather his elect to make up this heavenly city. The rising sun was considered an appropriate expression of this eschatological hope.

In the New Testament, the special significance of the eastward direction for worship is not explicit. Even so, tradition has found many biblical references for this symbolism, for instance, the sun of righteousness (Mal 4:2), the feet of the Lord standing on the Mount of Olives, which lies before Jerusalem on the east (Zech 14:4), the day dawning from on high (Lk 1:78), the angel ascending from the rising of the sun with the seal of the living God (Rev 7:2), not to mention the Johannine light imagery. According to early Christian exegesis, the sign of the coming of the Son of Man with power and great glory, which appears as lightning from the east and shines as far as the west, is the Cross (Mt 24:27 and 30).

Erik Peterson has shown the close connection of eastward prayer and the Cross, which is evident for the post-Constantinian period at the latest. In contemporary synagogues, the corner with the receptacle for the Torah scrolls indicated the direction of prayer (*qibla*) towards Jerusalem. The

---

[19] This is brought home by Wallraff, *Christus verus sol*, 60: 'Christen beten nach Osten. Dieser Grundsatz war der gesamten Alten Kirche eine Selbstverständlichkeit. Die Zeugnisse dafür sind räumlich und zeitlich breit gestreut. Nirgends findet sich ein Indiz für Christentum ohne diesen Brauch oder mit dem Brauch einer anderen Gebetsrichtung.'

seven-armed *menorah* and the sacrifice of Isaac could be depicted above this Torah shrine, as in the great synagogue of Dura-Europos from the first half of the third century. Among Christians, it became a general custom to mark the direction of prayer with a cross on the east wall in the apse of basilicas as well as in the private rooms of, for example, monks and solitaries.[20]

In this context, the direction of prayer in Islam is worthy of note. At first Muhammad followed the Jewish custom of praying towards Jerusalem. Later his attitude towards Judaism changed, not least because his preaching met with no great success among Jews, and he adopted elements of the ancient Arabic tradition. In the year 624 Muhammad prescribed that the ritual prayer of Muslims (*salat*) must be directed strictly towards the Kaaba of Mecca.[21] Islamic controversialists would later condemn the Christian custom of facing east in prayer as a relapse into sun worship. Before the introduction of a prayer niche (*mihrab*) in mosques, the Islamic *qibla* was indicated by special stones, similar to the marking by a cross of the east wall in Christian places of worship.[22]

Let us now turn to the literary sources for the Christian principle of praying towards the east. There is strong evidence for eastward prayer from most parts of the Christian world from the second century onwards. We shall consider

[20] See Peterson, *Frühkirche, Judentum und Gnosis*, 10–14 and 15–35; see also Vogel, 'La Croix eschatologique'.

[21] G. Monnot, 'Salāt', in *Encyclopédie de l'Islam*, ed. C. E. Bosworth, E. van Donzel, B. Lewis, and C. Pellat, new ed. (Leiden and Paris: Brill, 1995), 8:964, observes that it would be hard to overstate the importance of the *qibla*.

[22] On the Islamic direction of prayer, see Dölger, *Sol salutis*, 185–86; Peterson, *Frühkirche, Judentum und Gnosis*, 12–13; A. J. Wensinck, 'Kibla I', in *Encyclopédie de L'Islam*, ed. C. E. Bosworth, E. van Donzel, B. Lewis, and C. Pellat, new ed. (Leiden and Paris: Brill, 1986), 5:84–85; and Monnot, 'Salāt'.

briefly the most important texts, which have been presented in Dölger's study.[23]

In the first vision of the *Shepherd of Hermas*, Hermas sees the second woman who appeared to him pass out of sight in the direction of the east. Dölger takes this as an indication that Hermas would have turned towards the east in prayer. This would correspond to the prevailing custom of Roman Christians around the middle of the second century.[24] In the apocryphal *Acts of Paul*, written by a presbyter from Asia Minor around A.D. 180, the last moments before the martyrdom of the Apostle are described as follows:

> Then Paul stood with his face to the east (πρὸς ἀνατολὰς) and lifted up his hands to heaven and prayed a long time.[25]

If Paul had had time to pray before his execution, he certainly would have turned to the east, even if this had not yet been a Christian custom, for he would have turned towards Jerusalem. But we can safely assume that the fictional account in the *Acts of Paul* reflects the current practice in Asia Minor of turning towards the rising sun in prayer. The acts of the martyrs from the middle of the third century also testify that in the hour of martyrdom Christians turned to pray.[26]

As far as North Africa is concerned, Tertullian, in his works *To the Nations* and *The Apology* from A.D. 197, bears witness to the fact that the Christians' turning towards the east in

---

[23] See Dölger, *Sol salutis*, 136–286. See also C. Vogel, 'Sol aequinoctialis: Problèmes et technique de l'orientation dans le culte chrétien', *RevSR* 36 (1962): 175–211, and 'L'Orientation vers l'Est du célébrant et des fidèles pendant la célébration eucharistique', *OrSyr* 9 (1964): 3–37.

[24] *Shepherd of Hermas*, Vision 1: GCS *Apost. Väter*, 2d ed., I, 1–4; note, however, that Wallraff, 'Die Ursprünge', 172, n. 10, rejects this interpretation as forced.

[25] *Martyrium Pauli* 5: ed. Lipsius 115, 13–14.

[26] Cf. Dölger, *Sol salutis*, 323–24.

prayer, both in the liturgy and in private prayer at home, was so self-evident that it did not need express justification.[27] Around the same time Clement of Alexandria offers the following theological reasons for praying towards the east in his *Miscellanies* (*Stromata*):

> And since the dawn (ἀνατολή) is an image of the day of birth, and from that point the light 'which has shone forth at first from the darkness' (τὸ φῶς ... ἐκ σκότους λάμψαν) increases, there has also dawned on those involved in dark- ness a day of the knowledge of truth. In correspondence with the manner of the sun's rising, prayers are made to- wards the sunrise in the east. Whence also the most ancient temples looked towards the west, that people might be taught to turn to the east when facing the images [of the gods].[28]

This text is full of biblical resonances. The phrase τὸ φῶς... ἐκ σκότους λάμψαν is from 2 Corinthians 4:6: 'For it is the God who said, "Let light shine out of darkness", who has shone in our hearts to give the light of the knowledge of the glory (δόξα) of God in the face of Christ.' Isaiah 9:2 (taken up in Mt 4:6) is evoked when Clement speaks of those who wander around in ignorance, but upon whom, with Christ, the day of the knowledge of truth has arisen. Finally, the text offers an interpretation of pagan temple worship as an ex- pectation of the true enlightenment through the glorious light of Christ that, just like the sun, rises in the east. Given the predilection for an allegorical interpretation of Scripture

---

[27] Tertullian, *Ad nationes*, I, 13: CSEL 20, 83–84, and *Apologeticum* 16, 9–11: CSEL 69, 43–44.

[28] Clement of Alexandria, *Stromata* VII, 7, 43, 6–7: GCS Clem. Alex. III, 32–33; trans. W. Wilson (*Ante-Nicene Fathers*), 437.

among Alexandrian exegetes, it is notable that Clement does not develop this symbolism further here.[29]

The New Testament canticle of Zechariah praises Christ as the rising sun or, rather, as the dawn from on high (ἀνατολὴ ἐξ ὕψους, Lk 1:78). Thus it takes up the Old Testament theme of sun and light as the symbol and proclamation of salvation: 'But for you who fear my name the sun of righteousness shall rise, with healing in its wings' (Mal 4:2—cf. Wis 5:6). In his literary dialogue with the Jew Trypho Justin Martyr has recourse to this motif:

> For the word of His truth and wisdom is more ardent and more light-giving than the rays of the sun, and sinks down into the depths of heart and mind. Hence also the Scripture said, 'His name shall rise up above the sun' [Ps 71 (72):17]. And again, Zechariah says, 'His name is the East [ἀνατολή]' [Zech 6:12 LXX].[30]

Dölger considers it very likely that Justin's interpretation of Scripture is drawn from Philo, or at least from the Hellenistic-Jewish tradition of exegesis that the latter represents. Melito of Sardis calls Christ 'King of heaven and creation's Captain, Sun of uprising (ἥλιος ἀνατολῆς) who appeared both to the dead in Hades and to mortals in the world, he also alone rose a Sun out of heaven.'[31]

The reasons for facing east in prayer are explained with great clarity by Origen, who was active in the first half of

---

[29] Dölger, *Sol salutis*, 148–49.

[30] Justin, *Dialogus cum Tryphone* 121,1–2: 240 Goodspeed; trans. G. Reith (*Ante-Nicene Fathers*), 252. The Masoretic text of Zechariah 6:12 reads 'branch' for 'east'; cf. H. Savon, 'Zacharie 6, 12, et les justifications patristiques de la prière vers l'orient', in *Ecclesia orans: Mélanges patristiques offerts au Père Adalbert G. Hamman, O.F.M.*, ed. V. Saxer [= *Aug* 20 (1980):] 319–33.

[31] Melito of Sardis, *Fragment 8b*, 4; ed. and trans. S. G. Hall, 73.

the third century in Alexandria and Caesarea maritima in Palestine.[32] For instance, he writes in his treatise *On Prayer* (ca. A.D. 231):

> And now we must add a few remarks on the direction in which we should face while praying. There are four cardinal points—north, south, east, and west. It should be immediately clear that the direction of the rising sun obviously indicates that we ought to pray inclining in that direction, an act which symbolizes the soul looking towards where *the true light* rises.[33]

The rationale Origen provides for orientation in Christian prayer repeats motifs that are found already in Alexandrian-Jewish exegesis. At the same time, his argument is imbued with the symbolism of the fourth Gospel which presents Christ as the light of the world.[34] The eastward position in prayer is taken for granted, for it belongs to that sort of ecclesial custom that must be observed, even though the meaning is not familiar to everyone. Origen attests that together with other rites the turning to the east was 'handed on and entrusted to us by the High Priest and his sons', that is, it has its origin with Christ and his apostles.[35] Dölger does not go too far when he concludes from his survey of texts that the Christian practice of prayer facing east reaches back at least into the early second century.

The eastward direction was also very important for death and burial. Gregory of Nyssa records how his saintly sister Macrina right before her death spoke only with Christ,

[32] Cf. Dölger, *Sol salutis*, 157–70, with many references.

[33] Origen, *De oratione* 32: GCS Orig. II, 400, 21–26; trans. J.J. O'Meara (Ancient Christian Writers), 136.

[34] Cf. *Contra Celsum* V, 30: GCS Orig. II, 31–32, and *Hom. in Gen.* I, 5: GCS Orig. VI, 7.

[35] *Hom. in Num.* V, 1: GCS Orig. VII, 26.14—27.3.

looking at him steadfastly, 'since her bed was aligned towards the sunrise'.[36] The wish to turn towards Christ who was to come again from the east led to the burial of the dead in the direction towards the sunrise, as is evident in the early Christian burial sites of Gaul, Italy, and North Africa.[37]

Two early Church orders are especially valuable sources for the Christian direction of prayer. The Syrian *Didascalia Apostolorum*, a fourth-century text that is based on a Greek original presumably from the early third century, rules about liturgical celebrations in church:

> For thus is it required that the presbyters shall sit in the eastern part of the house with the bishops, and afterwards the laymen, and then the women; so that when you stand up to pray, the leaders may stand first, and after them the laymen, and then also the women. Indeed, it is required that you pray toward the east, as knowing that which is written: 'Give glory to God, who rides upon the heaven of heavens toward the east' (Ps 67[68]:34).[38]

Thus the whole liturgical assembly should turn towards the east in prayer. The psalm verse adduced to authenticate this rule is understood as a prophecy of the Lord's Ascension. Christ ascended towards the east, the place of paradise (Gen 2:8),[39] from where his Second Coming is expected. A close connection was perceived between the Ascension of Jesus and the hope for his Parousia, which found vivid expression

[36] Gregory of Nyssa, *Vita S. Macrinae*: PG 46, 984B.

[37] Dölger, *Sol salutis*, 258–72, where he also discusses the orientation of the tomb of Christ; see now also Wallraff, *Christus verus sol*, 78–79.

[38] *Didascalia Apostolorum* 12: CSCO 407, 144; trans. A. Vööbus (CSCO 408), 131. See also the revision of the Syrian *Didascalia* in the *Constitutiones Apostolorum* (between A.D. 375 and 400), II, 57, 14: SC 320, 316.

[39] Eastward prayer was taken to express a longing for paradise, see Dölger, *Sol salutis*, 220–42.

in the early Christian exclamations 'Come, Lord Jesus' (Rev
22:20) and 'Our Lord, come' (*Maranatha*, I Cor 16:22).[40]
That eastward prayer had an eschatological significance is
obvious from the first canon of the Syrian *Didascalia Addai*
(probably from the second quarter of the fourth century), as
F. C. Burkitt pointed out:[41]

> The apostles therefore appointed that you should pray to-
> wards the east, because 'as the lightning which lightens from
> the East and is seen even to the West, so shall the coming of
> the Son of man be' (Mt 24:27). By this may we know and
> understand that he will appear suddenly from the east.[42]

These two texts are all the more informative since they do
not present the thought of an individual theologian but, rather,
establish a general rule by appeal to tradition. As in Origen
this tradition is explained by reference to the apostles. Dölger
comments that the canon of the *Didascalia Addai* conveys the
impression of antiquity by its strongly pronounced hope for
the Lord's Second Coming. Compared with the *Didascalia
Apostolorum*, it is distinguished by greater clarity and simplicity befitting the form of the law.[43]

---

[40] Cf. ibid., 198–219: 'Die älteste Begründung der christlichen Gebets-
Ostung'.

[41] F. C. Burkitt, review of Dölger, *Sol salutis*, *JThS* 22 (1921): 283. A. Vööbus, 'New Light on the Text of the Canons in the Doctrine of Addai', *Journal
of the Syriac Academy* 1 (1975): 3–4, stresses the archaic character of these canons. On matters of origin and dating, see now W. Witakowski, 'The Origin of
the "Teaching of the Apostles"', in *IV Symposium Syriacum 1984*, OCA 229
(Rome: Pontificium Institutum Orientalium, 1987), 161–71, who
regards the text as a Syrian original from the second quarter of the fourth
century.

[42] *Didascalia Addai*, can. 1: CSCO 367, 201; trans. Burkitt, review of Dölger,
283 (modified).

[43] Dölger, *Sol salutis*, 179; cf. Burkitt, review of Dölger, 283: 'It is . . . of the
first importance to notice that the use of Matt. xxiv 27 in this connexion has

In the liturgy of the eighth book of the late fourth-century *Apostolic Constitutions*, which is based on the text of the so-called *Apostolic Tradition*, after the dismissals, the general prayer of the faithful (which was said kneeling), and the kiss of peace, the deacon proclaims: 'Let us stand upright before the Lord with fear and trembling, to offer the oblation.'[44] It is likely that this would include turning towards the east. By comparison, Greek, Coptic, and Ethiopian liturgies have similar diaconal exhortations to stand upright and look towards the east at the beginning or during the anaphora.[45] In the Egyptian liturgy of Saint Mark the deacon announces before the introduction to the *Trisagion*: 'You who are seated, stand up . . . attend to the east'.[46]

---

nothing whatever to do with Sun-worship: the Syriac Canon as it stands is a relic of the eschatological hopes of the early Christians and belongs to the Jewish environment in which Christianity was born, before it was ever contaminated (if it was contaminated) with heathen ideas and customs.'

[44] Ὀρθοὶ πρὸς Κύριον μετὰ φόβου καὶ τρόμου ἐστῶτες ὦμεν προσφέρειν, *Constitutiones Apostolorum* VIII, 12, 2: SC 336, 176.

[45] Dölger, *Sol salutis*, 327–30; see also M. J. Moreton, 'Εἰς ἀνατολὰς βλέψατε: Orientation as a Liturgical Principle', *StPatr* 18 (1982): 575–90.

[46] Apart from fragments dating from the fourth or fifth century, the earliest complete manuscripts we have of the liturgy of Saint Mark were copied in the thirteenth century, as O. Nußbaum, 'Die Zelebration versus populum und der Opfercharakter der Messe', *ZKTh* 93 (1971): 154–55, points out; see also the critical edition of G. J. Cuming, *The Liturgy of St Mark, Edited from the Manuscripts with a Commentary*, OCA 234 (Rome: Pontificium Institutum Studiorum Orientalium, 1990), 36 and 118. The most ancient fragments do not contain the relevant section of the anaphora where we would expect the exhortation Εἰς ἀνατολὰς βλέψατε. Despite this lack of evidence, however, an early date for it would seem likely. The case is similar with the Coptic anaphora of Saint Gregory. The papyrus fragment P. Vindob. K. 4854 from the second half of the sixth century attests the first word of the diaconal admonition 'Let us offer (προσφέρειν)', to which the manuscript tradition from the twelfth or thirteenth century adds: 'Stand upright, attend to the east.' The fragment is now available in an annotated edition by J. Henner, *Fragmenta Liturgica Coptica: Editionen und Kommentar liturgischer Texte der Koptischen Kirche des ersten*

In his catechetical homilies given before A.D. 392, Theodore of Mopsuestia mentions the diaconal admonition before the anaphora: 'Attend to the offering.'[47] This by no means implies that the celebrant faces the people so that the offertory gifts are visible. In an oriented church, as was the rule in Syria at this time, the admonition corresponds to the 'Attend to the east' of the liturgy of Saint Mark and other oriental anaphoras. The deacon exhorts the faithful to turn reverently towards the eastward-facing altar, where the eucharistic sacrifice is being offered.[48] Robert F. Taft maintains that in the dialogue preceding the anaphora, common to all liturgical traditions, the response 'Habemus ad Dominum' that follows the invitation 'Sursum corda' implies that the congregation would face east. In the early Church, this lifting up of hearts was accompanied by expressive bodily gestures: standing upright, raising one's arms, looking upward, and, most likely, turning towards the east.[49] Augustine asso-

---

Jahrtausends, Studien und Texte zu Antike und Christentum 5 (Tübingen: Mohr Siebeck, 2000), 42 and 48–50. Henner argues that the longer form of the diaconal admonition was used already in the sixth century. Since the papyrus transmits only the liturgical texts for the priest, the deacon's text was abbreviated and just the first word was written down.

[47] Theodore of Mopsuestia, *Hom. cat.* XV, 44–45, and XVI, 2:529–31 and 537 Tonneau-Devreesse.

[48] K. Gamber, *Liturgie und Kirchenbau: Studien zur Geschichte der Meßfeier und des Gotteshauses in der Frühzeit*, SPLi 6 (Regensburg: Pustet, 1976), 8, *pace* O. Nußbaum, *Der Standort des Liturgen am christlichen Altar vor dem Jahre 1000: Eine archäologische und liturgiegeschichtliche Untersuchung*, Theoph 18 (Bonn: Hanstein, 1965), 1:117–18. Cf. R. F. Taft, 'Textual Problems in the Diaconal Admonition before the Anaphora in the Byzantine Tradition', *OCP* 49 (1983): 365: 'The offering to which we must attend is the eucharist *tout court*.'

[49] R. F. Taft, 'The Dialogue before the Anaphora in the Byzantine Eucharistic Liturgy, II: The *Sursum corda*', *OCP* 54 (1988): 74–75; for different interpretations, see Nußbaum, 'Die Zelebration versus populum', 155, and Vogel, 'Sol aequinoctialis', 180–81, who thinks that the facing east, being implied in

ciates the lifting up of the heart with a complete turning towards Christ and the Kingdom of heaven. This may well entail a physical turning towards the east.[50]

Many of Augustine's sermons conclude with a prayer that is introduced in the manuscript tradition by short formulas such as *Conversi* (*ad Dominum*). At times this prayer is written out, as, for instance, in the following sermon:

> Let us turn towards the Lord God and Father Almighty, and with a pure heart let us give him abundant thanks as well as our littleness will allow. Let us with all our hearts and minds beseech his extraordinary clemency, so that he may vouchsafe to hear our prayers according to his good pleasure. May he by his power drive the enemy far from our acts and thoughts. May he multiply our faith, rule our mind, give us spiritual thoughts, and lead us to his blessedness, through Jesus Christ his Son. Amen.[51]

---

the dialogue, was demanded only of the celebrant. This appears most unlikely, since the response, 'Habemus ad Dominum', is given by the whole congregation.

[50] Augustine, *Sermo Dolbeau* 17, 6 and 21, 18: ed. F. Dolbeau, *Augustin d'Hippone: Vingt-Six Sermons au Peuple d'Afrique retrouvés à Mayence*, Collection des Études Augustiniennes, Série Antiquité 147 (Paris: Institut d'Études Augustiniennes, 1996), 146 and 296. The unusual form 'Sursum cor' is characteristic of Augustine.

[51] 'Conversi ad Dominum Deum Patrem omnipotentem, puro corde ei, quantum potest parvitas nostra, maximas atque uberes gratias agamus; precantes toto animo singularem mansuetudinem eius, ut preces nostras in beneplacito suo exaudire dignetur; inimicum a nostris actibus et cogitationibus sua virtute expellat, nobis multiplicet fidem, gubernet mentem, spirituales cogitationes concedat, et ad beatitudinem suam perducat: per Iesum Christum Filium eius. Amen': Augustine, *Sermo* 67: PL 38, 437; further references in Dölger, *Sol salutis*, 331–32. The formula *Conversi ad Dominum* at the end of the sermon is also found in Fulgentius and Caesarius of Arles, cf. M. Klöckener, 'Conuersi ad dominum', *AugL* 1 (1994): 1280–82, and F. Dolbeau, 'L'Oraison "Conuersi ad dominum …": Un Bilan provisoire des recensions existantes', *ALW* 41 (1999): 295–322.

The prayer *Conversi ad Dominum* at the end of the sermon summoned the faithful to turn eastward, as is evident from one of Augustine's sermons:

> Does God not say, 'Be converted to me'? The scriptures are full of it: 'Be converted to me, be converted to me.'[52] Indolence is beginning to be stirred. For what does this mean: 'Be converted to me'? It does not just mean that you, who were looking toward the west, should now look toward the east—that is easily done. If only you also did it inwardly, because that is not easily done. You turn your body around from one cardinal point to another; turn your heart around from one love to another.[53]

It is easy to turn from west to east physically, but it is not so easy to turn to the Lord with one's whole heart. Augustine is concerned that the inner disposition correspond to the external gesture. As in the liturgy, so in their everyday life the faithful must be directed towards Christ in charity.[54] Facing east in prayer was a well-established custom in North Africa, as Augustine makes clear in his discourse on the Ser-

---

[52] For example, Prov 1:23; Is 45:22; Jer 3:14, 22; Ezek 18:30, 33:11; Joel 2:12; Zech 1:3; Mal 3:7.

[53] 'Nonne deus dicit: *Convertimini ad me*? Plenae sunt scripturae. *Convertimini ad me, convertimini ad me*. Coepit enim movere languor. Quid est enim: *Convertimini ad me*? Non enim—quod facile fit—, qui adtendebas occidentem, adtendas orientem. Utinam hoc intus facias, quia hoc <non> est facile! Convertis corpus ex cardine in cardinem: cor converte ex amore in amorem': Augustine, *Sermo Dolbeau* 19, 12: Dolbeau, *Augustin d'Hippone*, 164.

[54] See Dolbeau, *Augustin d'Hippone*, 171–75; M. Klöckener, 'Die Bedeutung der neu entdeckten Augustinus-Predigten (*Sermones Dolbeau*) für die liturgiegeschichtliche Forschung', in *Augustin Prédicateur (395–411): Actes du Colloque International de Chantilly (5–7 septembre 1996)*, ed. G. Madec, Collection des Études Augustiniennes, Série Antiquité 159 (Paris: Institut d'Études Augustiniennes, 1998), 153–54; *pace* N. Duval, 'Commentaire topographique et archéologique', in Madec, *Augustin Prédicateur*, 196–98.

mon on the Mount: '[W]hen we stand at prayer, we turn to the east.'[55]

The symbolism of liturgical orientation is manifest in the baptismal rite, as described in the mystagogical catecheses of the fourth century, for example, by Ambrose of Milan, Cyril of Jerusalem, and Theodore of Mopsuestia. In the *apotaxis* the catechumen turns towards the west in order to renounce Satan and then performs a bodily conversion towards the east in order to give himself over to Christ.[56]

At the end of the patristic age, theologians of different traditions are found to agree that prayer facing east is one of the distinctive practices that mark Christianity out from the other religions of the Middle East. It is of singular importance in the East Syrian ('Nestorian') tradition. The outstanding Catholicos-Patriarch of the Church of the East, Timothy I (728–823), defends the eastward direction in his apology for Christianity before the Caliph Mahdi. Timothy argues that this custom was laid down by Christ himself:

> He [Christ] has taught us all the economy of the Christian religion: baptism, laws, ordinances, prayers, worship in the direction of the east, and the sacrifice that we offer. All these things He practised in His person and taught us to practise ourselves.[57]

At the request of the Catholicos-Patriarch Yahballaha III, the East Syrian theologian Abdisho (Ebedjesus) bar Brika

---

[55] Augustine, *De sermone domini in monte* II, 5, 18: CChr.SL 35, 108.

[56] The seminal study of F. J. Dölger, *Die Sonne der Gerechtigkeit und der Schwarze: Eine religionsgeschichtliche Studie zum Taufgelöbnis*, LF 2 (Münster: Aschendorff, 1918), is still instructive; see now also B. Kleinheyer, *Sakramentliche Feiern I: Die Feiern der Eingliederung in die Kirche*, GdK 7/1 (Regensburg: Pustet, 1989), 89–90, and Wallraff, *Christus verus sol*, 66–69.

[57] Timothy, *Apology for Christianity*: ed. A. Mingana, *The Apology of Timothy the Patriarch before the Caliph Mahdi*, Wood St, vol. 2, 1 (Cambridge: W. Heffer and Sons, 1928), 29.

(died 1318), metropolitan of Nisibis and Armenia, wrote a
short treatise on the truth of Christianity for catechetical purposes called the *Book of the Pearl (Marganitha)*. In the fifth
part of the book, which is entitled 'On the Theory of Those
Things that Prefigure the World to Come', the first chapter
is dedicated to worship towards the east, and only then follow
the chapters on the worship of the Lord's Cross and on the
observance of Sunday and of festivals of the Lord.[58]

The West Syrian ('Monophysite') tradition equally considers prayer facing east one of the characteristic features of
the Christian faith. Moses bar Kepha (815–903) in his short
*Treatise on the Unwritten Mysteries that Have Been Received and
Are Carried Out in Holy Church according to the Tradition of the
Holy Fathers* reckons the custom of turning eastward among
the 'mysteries (*roze*) of the Church'.[59]

Saint John of Damascus (died ca. 750), the great synthetic
thinker of the Eastern Church, provides an explanation of
the Christian direction of prayer in the concluding part of his
major work *On the Orthodox Faith*.[60] In place of a summary of
what has been said I should like to quote this text in full:

> It is not without reason or by chance that we worship to-
> wards the east. But seeing that we are composed of a visible
> and an invisible nature, of a nature partly of spirit and partly
> of sense, we render also a twofold worship to the Creator;

[58] Abdisho bar Brika, *Marganitha* V, 1: ed. G. P. Badger, *The Nestorians and
Their Rituals* (1852; reprint, London: Darf, 1987), 2:413–14.

[59] This unedited treatise by Moses bar Kepha is cited by W. de Vries, *Die
Sakramententheologie bei den syrischen Monophysiten*, OCA 125 (Rome: Pontificium Institutum Orientalium Studiorum, 1940), 30, on the basis of a sixteenth-
century manuscript owned by a Syrian Orthodox priest in Beirut.

[60] Cf. A. Louth, *St John Damascene: Tradition and Originality in Byzantine
Theology*, Oxford Early Christian Studies (Oxford: Oxford University Press,
2002), 179–80 and 182–83.

just as we sing both with our spirit and with our bodily lips, and are baptized with both water and Spirit, and are united with the Lord in a twofold manner, being sharers in the mysteries and in the grace of the Spirit. Since, therefore, God is spiritual light, and Christ is called in the Scriptures 'Sun of righteousness' [Mal 4:2] and 'Dayspring' [Zech 3:8, 6:12 LXX; Lk 1:78], the east is the direction that must be assigned to his worship. For everything good must be assigned to him from whom every good thing arises. Indeed the divine David also says, 'Sing to God, O kingdoms of the earth; sing praises to the Lord, to him who rides upon the heaven of heavens towards the east' [Ps 67:33–34 LXX]. Moreover the Scripture also says, 'And God planted a garden in Eden, in the east; and there he put the man whom he had formed' [Gen 2:8]; and when he had transgressed his command he expelled him and made him to dwell over against the delights of Paradise, which clearly is the west. So, then, we worship God seeking and striving after our old fatherland.... Moreover Christ, when he hung on the Cross, had his face turned towards the west, and so we worship, striving after him. And when he was received again into heaven he was borne towards the east, and thus his apostles worship him, and thus he will come again in the way in which they beheld his going towards heaven; as the Lord himself said, 'As the lightning comes from the east and shines as far as the west, so will be the coming of the Son of Man' [Mt 24:27]. So, then, in expectation of his coming we worship towards the east. But this tradition of the apostles is unwritten. For much that has been handed down to us by tradition is unwritten.[61]

---

[61] John of Damascus, *Expositio fidei* 85 (IV, 12): ed. Kotter, 190–91; trans. S. D. F. Salmond (*Nicene and Post-Nicene Fathers*), 81 (modified). The spiritual dimension of facing east in prayer is elucidated from the perspective of the Church Fathers by G. Bunge, *Earthen Vessels: The Practice of Personal Prayer according to the Patristic Tradition*, trans. M. J. Miller (San Francisco: Ignatius Press, 2002), 57–71.

When Saint Thomas Aquinas discusses the practice of praying towards the east, he does not refer to its apostolic origin but, rather, speaks of its 'fittingness' (*secundum quandam decentiam*), for which he provides three reasons:

> To adore facing east is fitting, first, because the movement of the heavens which manifest the divine majesty is from the east. Secondly, paradise was situated in the east according to the Septuagint version of Genesis, and we seek to return to paradise. Thirdly, because of Christ, who is *the light of the world* and is called *the Orient, who mounteth above the heaven of heaven to the east,* and is expected to come from the east according to Matthew, *as lightning comes out of the east, and shines even to the west, so also will the coming of the Son of Man be.*[62]

We can still recognise here the eschatological foundation for the eastward direction of prayer which is so prominent in the documents from the early Church.[63]

2. The Direction of Prayer and the Position of the Celebrant at the Altar

Facing east in prayer became decisive for early Christian liturgy and church architecture. As a rule, the eastward direction determined the position of the celebrant at the altar.

---

[62] Thomas Aquinas, *S. Th.* II–II, q. 84, a. 3 ad 3; Blackfriars trans., 111. The scriptural references given are Jn 8:12; Zech 6:12 (Vg.); Ps 67:34 (Vg.); Mt 24:27.

[63] J. A. Jungmann, *Liturgisches Erbe und pastorale Gegenwart: Studien und Vorträge* (Innsbruck: Tyrolia, 1960), 7, points to the eschatological quality of early Christian art. See also E. Keller, *Eucharistie und Parusie: Liturgie- und theologiegeschichtliche Untersuchungen zur eschatologischen Dimension der Eucharistie anhand ausgewählter Zeugnisse aus frühkirchlicher und patristischer Zeit,* SF NF 70 (Fribourg: Universitätsverlag 1989).

This has been the outcome of the discussion about Otto Nußbaum's comprehensive study of the pertinent literary and archaeological sources in the first millennium. Nußbaum summarises the results of his research as follows:

> Where the entrance was in the east, the altar was always placed between the celebrant and the congregation. Where the apse was in the east, in the early days both the celebrant's position *versus populum* and with his back to the people were evenly practised. It would seem that at first the orientation of the entrance and the orientation of the apse were on a par. Hence it can be inferred that since the first proper buildings for worship were constructed, there had been no strict rule as to on which side of the altar the celebrant was supposed to stand. He could just as well have stood either in front of or behind the altar. When from the beginning of the fifth century the type of church with an eastward-facing apse became the norm, this did not at once change the two existing possibilities of the direction of celebrant and congregation. It was only at a later point that the position of the celebrant in churches with the apse in the east came almost always to be between the congregation and the altar.[64]

According to Nußbaum, in the earliest known church buildings of Syria and Greece, the celebrating priest stood between the congregation and the altar, facing the apse. However, in other regions, such as Egypt and Italy, the position of the celebrant facing the people used to be the early practice and had become an exception only in the course of time. If this is a correct interpretation of the archaeological data, it is safe to conclude that, contrary to the clear-cut picture that is often presented, the priest did not in general stand facing the people during the celebration of the Eucharist

[64] Translating Nußbaum, *Der Standort des Liturgen*, 1:408.

in Christian antiquity. Moreover, where this was done, there was no 'turning towards the people' in the modern sense. However, we need to go one step further. Scholars have criticised Nußbaum's interpretation of the available sources as highly questionable.[65] One of the most important contributions to the debate is that of Marcel Metzger, and I shall present his rigorous criticism of Nußbaum's argument in the following section.

First of all, Metzger contends that, with regard to the position of the celebrant at the altar, the burden of proof lies with those who argue for a celebration facing the people. The practice of the patristic age can only be established if we have at our disposal clear data about the arrangement of early Christian sanctuaries. In fact, the majority of churches investigated by Nußbaum (some 360 of 560) give no indication of the celebrant's position. This is either because there are no traces of the original altar or because the altar could have been used on both sides. For any assertion about the layout and the use of the altar in these buildings, one is bound to start from working hypotheses. For instance, Jean Lassus and Georges Tchalenko assumed that the churches in any given region were similar in their architectural structure. Proceeding from the remaining monuments, they concluded in their research on ancient churches in Syria and Mesopotamia that the celebrant at the altar was generally facing the apse, which was directed towards the east.[66]

The weakness of Nußbaum's argument lies in his hypothesis that the celebration of the Eucharist facing the people

---

[65] J. A. Jungmann, review of O. Nußbaum, *Der Standort des Liturgen am christlichen Altar vor dem Jahre 1000*, *ZKTh* 88 (1966): 445–50; and 'Der neue Altar', 376: 'Die oft wiederholte Behauptung, daß der altchristliche Altar regelmäßig die Wendung zum Volke voraussetzte, erweist sich als Legende.'

[66] M. Metzger, 'La Place des liturges à l'autel', *RevSR* 45 (1971): 113–17.

must be taken for granted, unless the plan of a church shows otherwise. He is often content with insinuating that everything in a church suggests the face-to-face position of priest and people or at least gives no indication to the contrary.[67] For example, he determines the use of an altar *versus populum* by the existence of a *cathedra* or a bench for the clergy in the apse. According to this theory the celebrant, when he sits in the apse, walks straight to the altar, and so is directed towards the people. Such a conclusion, however, is in no way compelling. The simple fact that the way from the *cathedra* to the apse side of the altar is shorter than the way to the people's side, cannot be taken as proof that the celebrant would stand behind the altar. An equally possible theory, at least for a church with an oriented apse, is that after receiving the offerings from the people the celebrant would stay at the western side of the altar and turn eastward for the anaphora. Nußbaum is at pains to decide in favour of a celebration *versus populum* as often as possible and fails to consider how little space would remain for the celebrant between the altar and the apse wall or the raised platform for the clergy. Sometimes he says some three feet (one metre) would be enough, sometimes even less, for example in the southern church of Faras in Nubia and in the church of Borasi in Dalmatia, where he allows less than one and a half feet (forty centimetres).[68] Thus Nußbaum arrives at the conclusion that in 192 of the

---

[67] For instance, Nußbaum, *Der Standort des Liturgen*, 1:78, 98, 186, 238, 289, and 290.

[68] Ibid., 95–96 and 303. Anne Michel concludes from her recent survey of ancient churches in Jordan: 'The altar placed on the chord of the apse generally left little space between it and the synthronon for the clergy to move about': A. Michel, *Les Églises d'époque byzantine et ummayyade de la Jordanie (provinces d'Arabie et de Palestine), Ve-VIIIe siècle: Typologie architecturale et aménagements liturgiques (avec catalogue des monuments)*, Bibliothèque de l'antiquité tardive 2 (Turnhout: Brepols, 2001), XII–XIII.

560 churches he examined, the altar can be used facing the people. By contrast, Metzger shows that this is the case for some twenty of the buildings in question.[69]

The rationale behind Nußbaum's giving systematic priority to the celebration *versus populum* is his theory that this was the original form of the Eucharist. Nußbaum thinks that the first Christians participated in the Liturgy of the Word in the Temple but celebrated the eucharistic banquet in their own houses. When the two forms of worship were eventually combined, it was customary for the presider to stand behind the holy table, turned towards the people like the speaker in front of an assembly. According to Nußbaum, only the later emphasis on the sacrificial character of the Eucharist led to the 'turning away' of the celebrant from the people. On a principal note, Metzger reminds us that any discussion about the celebration of the Eucharist in the primitive Church is purely hypothetical, since the literary sources are extremely reticent and no archaeological monuments have come down to us. The celebration of the Eucharist was not invented *ex nihilo*; rather, it was taken from elements of contemporary ritual banquets, Jewish as well as pagan. There is no warrant to derive the earliest form of the Eucharist from the customs used at ordinary meals. The contemporary Jewish meal celebrations in particular provide the context for Jesus and his apostles, immersed as they were in this tradition. It would be fallacious to imagine some kind of primitive creativity that was later lost. This does not of course mean that one can simplistically derive the Eucharist from any or all of these forms, since it was, after all, a new reality.[70]

---

[69] Metzger, 'Place des liturges à l'autel', 117–19.

[70] Ibid., 119–21.

It is widely believed that at the Last Supper our Lord and his apostles would have followed contemporary custom and sat (or more likely reclined) on the convex side of a semi-circular shaped table, leaving the other side free for serving the food.[71] The place of honour was not in the middle but on the right of the semicircle (*in cornu dextro*). This arrangement is depicted in the oldest representations of the Last Supper in mosaics and book illuminations from the fifth century far into the Middle Ages (fig. 1).[72] It would seem natural that the primitive Christians retained the traditions of the Upper Room where the Lord instituted the Eucharist. When the eucharistic banquet was celebrated in private houses, the presider presumably took the place of Jesus Christ on the right side. On the occasion of larger gatherings the Eucharist was celebrated separately from the community meal, so that now only one table was needed for the presider. However, we must insert a caveat here, for we cannot simply conceive of the Last Supper as the exclusive model for the ritual shape of the Eucharist. And even if the community meal was the original form of the Eucharist, the development of the first centuries towards a liturgical rite cannot be undone.

Nußbaum suggests that the proclamation of the Word of God and the celebration of the Eucharist were originally

---

[71] It should be added that no single large table was used but rather a number of small three- or four-legged tables, holding food and dishes for one or two persons; cf. H. G. Thümmel, 'Versammlungsraum, Kirche, Tempel', in *Gemeinde ohne Tempel/Community without Temple: Zur Substituierung und Transformation des Jerusalemer Tempels und seines Kults im Alten Testament, antiken Judentum und frühen Christentum*, ed. B. Ego, A. Lange, P. Pilhofer, K. Ehlers, WUNT 118 (Tübingen: Mohr Siebeck, 1999), 490–91.

[72] Nußbaum, *Der Standort des Liturgen*, 1:373–76; K. Gamber, *The Modern Rite: Collected Essays on the Reform of the Liturgy*, trans. H. Taylor (Farnborough: Saint Michael's Abbey Press, 2002), 26; Bouyer, *Liturgy and Architecture*, 53–54.

Figure 1. The Last Supper as depicted on a mosaic in S. Apollinare Nuovo, Ravenna (around 520).

separate. Metzger objects that this hypothesis is not well grounded, although it gained some currency among students of the early liturgy. The eucharistic banquet was held κατ' οἶκον (Acts 2:46 and 5:42), that is, in a suitable house with a spacious dining room;[73] this is likely to have been the place of Scripture readings and religious instruction as well. The primitve Christians may well have gone to the synagogue on the Sabbath, but they celebrated the Eucharist on the first day of the week. It would seem plausible to assume that the eucharistic banquet was preceded by readings and preaching, after

[73] In addition to the Upper Room in Jerusalem (ὑπερῷον in Acts 1:13; ἀνάγαιον in Mark 14:15 and Luke 22:12) the New Testament speaks, for instance, of the house in Troas (Acts 20:7–12), the house of Prisca and Aquila in Rome (Rom 16:3–5), and of the house of Gaius in Corinth (Rom 16:23).

the manner of the synagogue services. This is at least as likely as the hypothesis of an original division between the two elements of the Christian liturgy.[74]

At any rate, we know far too little about the position of the celebrant at the altar for the first two hundred years to give a definitive answer. Nußbaum's hypothesis that the change in emphasis from meal to sacrifice in the understanding of the Eucharist, taking place around 400, resulted in the celebrant's turning away from the people is undermined by very early documents, such as the *Didache* and the *First Letter of Clement* (ca. 100), where the celebration of the Eucharist is clearly perceived as sacrificial.[75] Given our inadequate knowledge of the Church's liturgy in the first three centuries, it would be flawed to see in the official recognition of Christianity by Emperor Constantine in 313 a decisive turning point in the theology of the Eucharist. Furthermore, the texts that Nußbaum adduces in favour

---

[74] Metzger, 'Place des liturges à l'autel', 121–22. Cf. Thümmel, 'Versammlungsraum, Kirche, Tempel', 489–90: 'Mahl und Predigt sind gewiß sehr bald in *einer* Versammlung zusammengefaßt gewesen', even if there were local differences.

[75] R. Meßner, 'Unterschiedliche Konzeptionen des Meßopfers im Spiegel von Bedeutung und Deutung der Interzessionen des römischen Canon missae', in *Das Opfer: Biblischer Anspruch und liturgische Gestalt*, ed. A. Gerhards and K. Richter, QD 186 (Freiburg: Herder, 2000), 129: 'Es besteht gar kein Zweifel an der Tatsache, daß der Gedanke eines "Meßopfers" in der frühchristlichen Exegese von Mal 1,11 wurzelt. Seit der Didache wird das "reine Opfer" . . . , durch das Gottes Name unter den Völkern verherrlicht wird . . . , auf die christliche Eucharistie gedeutet'. See also K. S. Frank, 'Maleachi 1, 10ff. in der frühen Väterdeutung: Ein Beitrag zu Opferterminologie und Opferverständnis in der alten Kirche', *ThPh* 53 (1978): 70–78, and G. G. Willis, *A History of Early Roman Liturgy to the Death of Pope Gregory the Great*, with a memoir of G. G. Willis by M. Moreton, HBS, Subsidia 1 (London: Boydell Press, 1994), 3–4.

of a celebration *versus populum*[76] do not allow for the conclusion that the faithful could observe what was happening on the altar. Even where the celebrant stood facing the people, they could scarcely have seen much, either because of the elaborate superstructure around the altar or because of the distance between the sanctuary and the nave in a large basilica. In the East, curtains were presumably drawn to veil the altar at certain parts of the liturgy.[77] Hence the idea that the Eucharist was originally celebrated *versus populum* would not appear to be a sound working hypothesis for explaining the layout of ancient churches. Metzger argues that a far more judicious way of accounting for the characteristics of early church architecture is to proceed from the liturgical principle of facing east, especially since the eastward direction of prayer was universally observed in early Christianity.[78]

We need not deal further with the literary sources that have been discussed above. Metzger concludes that most of the churches described by Nußbaum that provide any information on the position of the celebrant, with exceptions in certain regions, suggest that the priest was generally facing east in the liturgy.[79] It comes as no surprise that no synodical

---

[76] Nußbaum, *Der Standort des Liturgen*, 1:24–30, 62–64, 87–90, 117–20, 134–37, 171–77, 216–21, 305–11.

[77] Ibid., 1:448, concedes: 'Eusebius, Zeno von Verona, Ambrosius und Augustinus sprechen zwar davon, daß die Gläubigen die innersten Geheimnisse auf dem Altar sehen können, aber in Wirklichkeit war das in vielen Kirchen des 4.–6. Jh. im Osten und im Westen sehr erschwert oder ganz unmöglich.'

[78] Metzger, 'Place des liturges à l'autel', 122–24.

[79] Of the 560 churches included in Nußbaum's study, 512 have an oriented apse (91.6 percent). Some 365 churches (65 percent) do not provide any specific evidence on the celebrant's position at the altar. In 173 churches the celebrant was obviously facing east, that is 31 percent of all the buildings in question and 88.7 percent of the buildings that in some way indicate the position of the celebrant. In twenty-two churches the celebrant could not face east owing to the layout of the building, that is, 4 percent of all the churches

canon is known that prescribes the celebrating priest's turning towards the east. Traditions are usually passed on through practice, whereas the point of a legal pronouncement lies mainly in modifying an existing usage or in evoking and confirming a custom that has been called into question or abused. The rules in the *Didascalia Apostolorum* and the *Didascalia Addai*, being presented with the claim of apostolic origin, can be read as an indication that already in the third century turning towards the east was an established use in Syria.[80]

Most ancient churches have an oriented apse, but there are also churches with an oriented entrance. According to Metzger, three points are to be considered here. First, the orientation of the apse was the prevailing custom. In fact, the number of churches with an eastward entrance is small; they can be found chiefly in Rome and North Africa. In the case of basilicas constructed over the tombs of saints, the site of these highly venerated *memoriae* determined the layout of the church and often did not allow the orientation of the apse. Several Roman basilicas are not aligned along the east–west axis for which different reasons can be found:[81] many churches rested on ancient foundations; already under Constantine secular buildings were turned to Christian use; in the majority of cases the variation from the east–west axis was owing to the constraints of the location, for the entrance to the church usually lay on the street side, as in the case of the church of San Clemente in Rome, where the doors open to the south-east. Secondly, the principle of

---

in question and 11.2 percent of the churches that in some way indicate the position of the celebrant.

[80] Metzger, 'Place des liturges à l'autel', 125–34.

[81] Cf. S. de Blaauw, *Met het oog op het licht: Een vergeten principe in de oriëntatie van het vroegchristelijk kerkgebouw*, Nijmeegse Kunsthistorische Cahiers 2 (Nijmegen: Nijmegen University Press, 2000), 17–23.

orientation was so dominant that there are regions where no churches with an eastward entrance can be found (Asia Minor, Greece, Noricum, and Dalmatia). Furthermore, churches that originally had a westward apse were often reordered at a later stage. Thirdly, the principle of facing east was so important that the celebrant in churches with an entrance in the east possibly turned to the nave (this point will be addressed below). All this adds up to the conclusion that it is the wrong question to ask, as Nußbaum does, at what time in any given region a transition was made from the celebration 'facing the people' to the priest's 'turning away' from the congregation.[82]

Finally, I should like to note that despite claims to the contrary there is no explicit evidence from the early Church that the altar as such was considered the focus of orientation in the liturgy.[83] That the altar was highly venerated can be substantiated as early as the fourth century; its holiness is based on the fact that on it the eucharistic sacrifice is immolated.[84] However, the overriding principle for the direction at prayer in the Eucharist is turning eastward, that is, facing the risen Christ who is to come again in glory.

---

[82] Metzger, 'Place des liturges à l'autel', 134–35. For a similar censure, see Gamber, *Modern Rite*, 29, and, with fuller documentation, Gamber, *Liturgie und Kirchenbau*, 7–27. Nußbaum's approach is also criticised by de Blaauw, *Met het oog op het licht*, 12–14, and Wallraff, *Christus verus sol*, 73, n. 55. De Blaauw points at Nußbaum's debt to the ideas of J. Braun, *Der christliche Altar in seiner geschichtlichen Entwicklung* (Munich: Alte Meister Guenther Koch, 1924), 1:412–16. A more recent example of this methodology is N. Duval, 'L'Architecture chrétienne et les pratiques liturgiques en Jordanie en rapport avec la Palestine: Recherches nouvelles', in '*Churches Built in Ancient Times': Recent Studies in Early Christian Architecture*, ed. K. Painter (London: Society of Antiquaries, 1994), 149–212, esp. 169–70, 177, and 203.

[83] This point is made by Gamber, *Modern Rite*, 30–31.

[84] Cf. the references given by Nußbaum, *Der Standort des Liturgen*, 1:402–3.

3. Liturgy and Church Architecture[85]

Even before the Constantinian settlement Christian communities had their own buildings dedicated to liturgical worship. The *Chronicle of Edessa* records for the year 201 that the 'sanctuary of the Church of Christ' in the city was destroyed by floods.[86] In the second half of the third century, Porphyry notes in his work *Against the Christians* that they imitate the construction of temples and build very large houses (μεγίστους οἴκους) in which they come together and pray.[87] This information is confirmed by Eusebius of Caesarea, who writes about the life of the Church in the late third century:

> But how can any one describe those vast assemblies, and the multitude that crowded together in every city, and the famous gatherings in the houses of prayer (προσευκτήρια); on whose account not being satisfied with the ancient buildings they erected from the foundation large churches (ἐκκλησίαι) in all the cities?[88]

---

[85] For a survey of recent scholarly literature, see S. de Blaauw, 'Architecture and Liturgy in Late Antiquity and the Middle Ages', *ALW* 33 (1991): 1–34; cf. also de Blaauw, *Met het oog op het licht.*

[86] *Chronicum Edessenum*: CSCO 1 (Scr. Syr. 3/4), 2–4. The reliability of this source is disputed by W. Bauer, *Orthodoxy and Heresy in Earliest Christianity*, trans. by a team from the Philadelphia Seminar on Christian Origins, ed. R. A. Kraft and G. Krodel (Philadelphia: Fortress Press, 1971), 12–14. However, his argument suffers from the *petitio principii* that there *cannot* have been specific buildings for Christian worship around the year 200.

[87] Porphyry, *Adversus Christianos*, fragment 76, ed. A. von Harnack, *Porphyrius 'Gegen die Christen', 15 Bücher: Zeugnisse, Fragmente und Referate*, APAW.PH 1 (Berlin: Königlich Akademie der Wissenschaften, in Kommission bei Georg Reimer, 1916), 93.

[88] Eusebius of Caesarea, *Hist. eccl.* VIII, 1, 5: GCS Euseb. II/2, 738; trans. A. C. McGiffert (*Ante-Nicene Fathers*), 323.

In fact, Eusebius presents the destruction of churches as a characteristic of the Diocletian persecution.[89] These pre-Constantinian churches could be well provided with precious altar plate, as emerges from the report of a confiscation in the church of Cirta in North Africa dated 19 May 303.[90]

One of the most significant archaeological discoveries in recent decades is the Christian building of Dura-Europos, a Roman frontier city on the river Euphrates. The city was almost completely destroyed by the Sassanians in A.D. 256 and was not rebuilt afterwards. Owing to this circumstance, the structure of a house church from the first half of the third century has been preserved (fig. 2). The assembly hall is oriented and has a platform on the east side, which might indicate the place of the altar.[91]

Apart from a few exceptions, the oldest extant monuments of church architecture date from the fourth century, when the official recognition of Christianity by the Emperor Constantine released a surge of building activity. The surviving Syrian churches mostly follow the model of the basilica, similar to contemporary synagogues, with the difference, however, that they were in general built with their apse facing towards the east. The archaeological finds in North Syria and Mesopotamia are especially informative.[92] Where

---

[89] Cf. Thümmel, 'Versammlungsraum, Kirche, Tempel', 492–93 and 499.

[90] The report from the *Acta Munati Felicis* is cited in the *Gesta apud Zenophilum*: CSEL 26, 187.

[91] C. H. Kraeling, *The Christian Building*, The Excavations at Dura Europos, Final Report 8, pt. 2 (New Haven: Dura-Europos Publications, 1967).

[92] J. Lassus, *Sanctuaires chrétiens de Syrie* (Paris: P. Geuthner, 1947), and 'La Liturgie dans les basiliques syriennes', in *Atti dell' VIII Congresso internazionale di studi bizantini: Palermo 3–10 aprile 1951*, Studi bizantini e neoellenici 8 (Rome: Associazione nazionale per gli studi bizantini, 1953), 418–28; G. Tchalenko, *Villages antiques de la Syrie du Nord: Le Massif du Bélus à l'époque romaine*, 3 vols. (Paris: P. Geuthner, 1953–1958); G. Tchalenko and E. Baccache, *Églises*

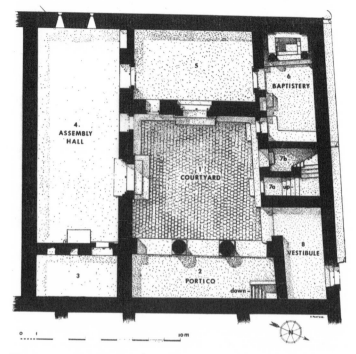

Figure 2. Ground plan (simplified) of the Christian building in Dura-Europos.

some clue remains as to the position of the altar (which is rare), it is placed only a little forward from the east wall or directly before it. The orientation of church and altar thus corresponds to the universally accepted principle of

de village de la Syrie du Nord, 2 vols. (Paris: P. Geuthner, 1979–1980); and G. Tchalenko, *Églises syriennes à bêma* (Paris: P. Geuthner, 1990). For a survey of scholarly research on early Syrian churches, see R. F. Taft, 'Some Notes on the Bema in the East and West Syrian Traditions', *OCP* 34 (1968): 326–59. Reprint with supplementary notes in R. F. Taft, *Liturgy in Byzantium and Beyond*, CStS 493 (Aldershot: Ashgate, 1995).

facing east in prayer and expresses the eschatological hope of the early Christians for the Second Coming of Christ as the Sun of righteousness.[93] The bema, a raised platform in the middle of the building, was taken over from the synagogue, where it served as the place for the reading of Holy Scripture and the recitation of prayers. In the East Syrian (Chaldean) rite the bishop sits with his clergy on the west side of the bema in the nave facing towards the apse. The psalmody and readings that form part of the Liturgy of the Word are conducted from the bema. The clergy then proceed eastward to the altar for the liturgy of the Eucharist (fig. 3).

Archaeological and literary sources show that this 'Syrian arrangement' existed in West Syrian churches as well, although it would seem that it was not adopted everywhere. Taft argues that in this region liturgical developments were usually passed on from west to east, so that the bema structure may well have spread from West Syria to Mesopotamia. It was retained in the East Syrian rite but was discarded in the area from which it had come.[94]

As for the origin of the bema, Bouyer observes that elements from Jewish worship were carried on longest among

[93] Where an existing edifice was adapted for liturgical purposes, the apse with the altar was constructed in the eastern part of the building, even though this was the long side and was not opposite the entrance. This is shown by a recently discovered church in Palmyra from the first half of the third century; cf. M. Gawlikowski, 'Eine neuentdeckte frühchristliche Kirche in Palmyra', in *Syrien: Von den Aposteln zu den Kalifen*, ed. E. M. Ruprechtsberger (Mainz: Von Zabern, 1993), 155–57.

[94] Taft, 'Some Notes on the Bema', 358; on the bema, see now also E. Renhart, *Das syrische Bema: Liturgisch-archäologische Untersuchungen*, GrTS 20 (Graz: Schnider, 1995).

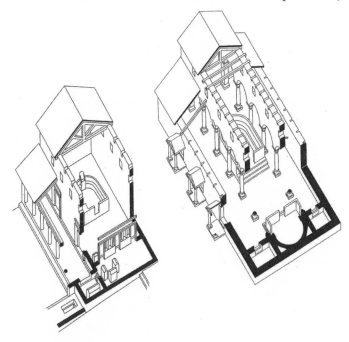

Figure 3. Early Syrian churches with a *bema*. Left the church of Qirqbīze (fourth century) with a single nave, right the basilica of Sinhār (mid-fourth century).

the Christians of the Near East.[95] Moreover, he rightly emphasises that these ancient churches must be studied in relation to contemporary synagogue architecture. The French theologian even supposes that the separation of the East Syrian Church from the Imperial Church in the fifth century was not primarily owing to the christological

[95] See also G. Rouwhorst, 'Jewish Liturgical Traditions in Early Syriac Christianity', *VigChr* 51 (1997): 72–93.

controversies but originated from the concern to preserve its semitic traditions, which were seen to be archaic already in patristic times. The East Syrians might have regarded the on-going Hellenisation of the Imperial Church as a threat to their native customs and practices.[96] Bouyer's theory that the 'Syrian arrangement' with the bema in the nave was also the original layout in the Byzantine rite has met with a very mixed reception among scholars.[97] Be this as it may, Syrian churches were generally oriented with the apse, and it is widely agreed that the celebrant would have stood in front of the altar, facing east with the congregation for the eucharistic liturgy.

The origins of early Roman church architecture have been the subject of much learned debate.[98] Many theories once popular have been rejected; for example, it is generally acknowledged today that the catacombs were not used for the liturgical assemblies of the early Christian communities. Long before the end of the persecutions, Christians in the city of Rome had their own buildings for the celebration of the liturgy, but as for the shape of these pre-Constantinian *tituli* or *domus ecclesiae*, we are very much in the dark.[99] The oldest

---

[96] Bouyer, *Liturgy and Architecture*, 24–39.

[97] Cf. the criticism of Taft, 'Some Notes on the Bema', 327 and 359.

[98] See Bouyer, *Liturgy and Architecture*, 39–60.

[99] Cf. C. Pietri, *Roma christiana: Recherches sur l'Église de Rome, son organisation, sa politique, son idéologie de Miltiade à Sixte III (311–440)*, BEFAR 224 (Rome: École française de Rome, 1976), 1:3–4; R. Krautheimer with S. Ćurčić, *Early Christian and Byzantine Architecture*, 4th ed. (New Haven and London: Yale University Press, 1986), 29; and F. Guidobaldi, 'L'inserimento delle chiese titolari di Roma nel tessuto urbano preesistente: Osservazioni ed implicazioni', in *Quaeritur inventus colitur: Miscellanea in onore di Padre U. M. Fasola* (Vatican City: Istituto di archeologia cristiana, 1989), 382–96. On the basis of the number of clergy listed in Pope Cornelius' letter to Bishop Fabius of Antioch (cited by Eusebius, *Hist. eccl.* VI, 43, 11), it is estimated that the Roman Church in the middle of the third century had between 30,000 and 50,000 faithful;

surviving monuments are the basilicas built under Constantine, but we should remember that the interior of these buildings has been changed considerably over the centuries. Arguably, the Constantinian plan can be discerned most clearly from the Lateran basilica. Here, the bishop's *cathedra* was placed at the end of the apse, which corresponded to the seat of honour occupied by the magistrate in secular basilicas, which were used as court or market halls, and to the Emperor's seat in the senate. As a result of the Constantinian settlement bishops enjoyed the same rank as high state officials and were invested with the same signs of honour. In the early Roman basilicas, the altar stood either at the entrance to the apse or in the central nave, its sacred character being marked by its exalted position, by the steps leading up to it, and by a ciborium, a superstructure that was particularly apt to emphasise the altar's importance.

There is no clear evidence for the original position of the main altar in the Constantinian building of Saint Peter's.[100] The Vatican basilica was a *martyrium*, marked out by the tomb of the Apostle, and its design was governed primarily, not by the needs of a liturgical assembly, but by the peculiar site of

---

cf. A. von Harnack, *The Mission and Expansion of Christianity in the First Three Centuries*, trans. and ed. J. Moffatt, 2d ed. (London and New York: Williams and Norgate, 1908), 2:247–48.

[100] The Emperor Constantine endowed Saint Peter's with an altar of silver chased with gold and weighing 350 pounds and rich altar plate, as recorded in the *Liber Pontificalis* 34: ed. Duchesne 1:176–77. The rather elusive passage from Jerome, *C. Vigilantium* 8: PL 23, 346B (361D–362A), written about 400, does not support any firm conclusions. Gregory of Tours transmits the impressions his deacon Agiulfus had of Saint Peter's towards the end of the pontificate of Pelagius II (579–590), speaking of a "sepulchrum sub altare collocatum": *Miraculorum libri I (De gloria martyrum)*: ed. B. Krusch (MGH.SRM 1/2), 504. Cf. A. Arbeiter, *Alt-St. Peter in Geschichte und Wissenschaft: Abfolge der Bauten, Rekonstruktion, Architekturprogramm* (Berlin: Mann, 1988), 181–84 and 204–6.

the *memoria*. As J.B. Ward-Perkins indicates, there would hardly have been room for the altar within the precinct of the tomb, let alone within the shrine itself.[101] Hence it is quite possible that the (portable) altar of the church was originally placed in the body of the nave and was not connected with Saint Peter's tomb, which would have been freely accessible to the faithful. Achim Arbeiter believes Saint Peter's was partitioned into two main areas: the nave, which served for the celebration of the Eucharist, and the transept with the shrine of the Apostle, which formed the sacred area for the pilgrims. The position of the altar may have been under the triumphal arch or in the nave, but not under the crossing.[102] On the other hand Sible de Blaauw argues that the main altar was in the area of the tomb (fig. 4).[103] Werner Jacobsen suggests that the altar stood near the tomb of Saint Peter and could be approached only from the side of the nave. This was owing to the second-century martyr shrine (*tropaion*) that was incorporated into the basilica to indicate the tomb of the Apostle. According to Jacobsen, the *tropaion* blocked the rear side of the altar, so that during the Eucharist the celebrant could only stand facing towards the apse, that is, westward.[104]

[101] J. Toynbee and J. Ward Perkins, *The Shrine of St. Peter and the Vatican Excavations* (London: Longmans, Green, 1956), 208, and J.B. Ward-Perkins, 'The Shrine of St. Peter and Its Twelve Spiral Columns', in *Studies in Roman and Early Christian Architecture* (London: Pindar Press, 1994), 470. Cf. Pietri, *Roma christiana*, 1:69: 'A notre connaissance, pas d'autel fixe: le monument grandiose s'organisait pour une zone sainte où Constantin et la piété romaine reconnaissaient la tombe de l'Apôtre.'

[102] Arbeiter, *Alt-St. Peter in Geschichte und Wissenschaft*, 204–5.

[103] S. de Blaauw, *Cultus et décor: Liturgia e architettura nella Roma tardoantica e medievale: Basilica Salvatoris, Sanctae Mariae, Sancti Petri* (Vatican City: Biblioteca Apostolica Vaticana, 1994), 2:481–82.

[104] W. Jacobsen, 'Organisationsformen des Sanktuariums im spätantiken und mittelalterlichen Kirchenbau: Wechselwirkungen von Altarraum und Liturgie aus kunsthistorischer Perspektive', in *Kölnische Liturgie und ihre Geschichte: Studien*

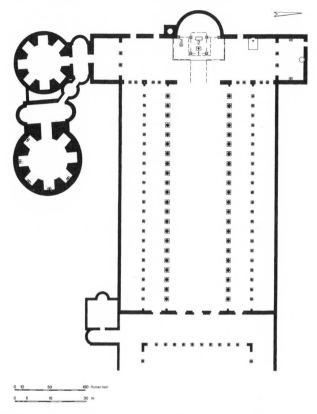

Figure 4. Ground plan of St. Peter's during the pontificate of Symmachus (498–514), according to S. de Blaauw, who locates the main altar within the precinct of the tomb.

1. Main altar
2. Tropaion with Confessio
3. Cathedra

zur interdisziplinären Erforschung des Gottesdienstes im Erzbistum Köln, ed. A. Gerhards and A. Odenthal, LWQF 87 (Münster: Aschendorff, 2000), 70–71.

At any rate, there is no doubt that the arrangement at the Apostle's tomb was changed significantly during the pontificate of Saint Gregory the Great (590–604).[105] The floor of the apse was raised by almost five feet (one and a half metres) and the elevated platform was extended nearly six and a half yards (six metres) into the body of the church. The altar with canopy was erected directly over the tomb, and on its western end a semicircular crypt was added that gave the faithful easy access to the highly venerated shrine. The curtains of the canopy served decorative purposes and emphasised the holiness of the action performed at the altar.[106] The raised apse with the bishop's throne and the bench for the clergy was separated from the body of the church by a screen of columns (fig. 5). Gregory the Great's primary motive for visibly uniting the altar with the *memoria* can be seen in the desire to respond to the strongly felt association between the celebration of the Eucharist and the cult of the martyrs.[107] It was also the Pope's intention to assimilate the plan of Saint Peter's to that of the Lateran basilica.[108]

Basilicas with an oriented entrance are found chiefly in Rome and North Africa, where the uses of the Roman church were closely followed. A fourth- or early fifth-century mosaic depicting the church of Thabarca in North Africa shows the altar standing more or less in the middle of the central

---

[105] The *Liber Pontificalis* 66: ed. Duchesne, 1:312, says: 'Hic fecit ut super corpus beati Petri missae celebrarentur.'

[106] Curtains did not have a liturgical function in the Latin West; see De Blaauw, *Cultus et décor*, 1:96–98.

[107] Cf. H. Brandenburg, 'Altar und Grab: Zu einem Problem des Märtyrerkultes im 4. und 5. Jh', in *Martyrium in Multidisciplinary Perspective: Memorial Louis Reekmans*, ed. M. Lamberigts and P. van Deun (Louvain: Peeters, 1995), 71–98.

[108] Cf. De Blaauw, *Cultus et décor*, 1:117–27, and Jacobsen, 'Organisationsformen des Sanktuariums', 71–72.

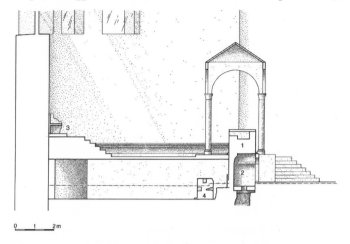

Figure 5. Longitudinal section (schematic) of the sanctuary of St. Peter's in the seventh century. The dotted line indicates the floor-level of the Constantinian apse.

1. The main altar of Gregory the Great
2. Confessio
3. Cathedra
4. Altar of the crypt

nave (fig. 6). Furthermore, a sermon preached by Augustine in the cathedral-basilica of Carthage clearly indicates that the altar was set a long way down the nave and was walled off by choir rails (*cancelli*).[109]

As for the direction of liturgical prayer in basilicas with the entrance in the east and the apse in the west, various

---

[109] Augustine, *Sermo Dolbeau 2 (de oboedientia)*, 3–4: ed. Dolbeau, *Augustin d'Hippone*, 329–30. Cf. Duval, 'Commentaire topographique et archéologique', 182. A good survey of the Dolbeau sermons is provided by H. Chadwick, 'New Sermons of St Augustine', *JThS* NS 47 (1996): 69–91.

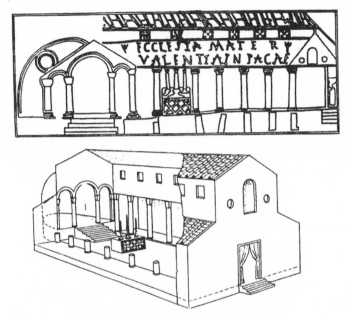

Figure 6. The mosaic of Thabarca and an axiometric reconstruction of the church according to J. B. Ward-Perkins and R. G. Goodchild.

hypotheses have been presented. According to Bouyer, the whole assembly, both the celebrant, who stood behind the altar, and the people in the nave, turned towards the east during the Eucharistic Prayer.[110] This suggestion has met severe criticism on the grounds that it would have been unthinkable for the people to turn their back on the altar, since from the earliest times the altar was considered a holy object,

---

[110] Bouyer, *Liturgy and Architecture*, 55–56.

indeed a symbol of Christ.[111] Gamber holds that the
congregation mainly occupied the side naves, of which Saint
Peter's and the Lateran had four and some churches even six.
The central nave would have been left free for liturgical
actions, such as the solemn entry of the celebrant and his
assistants and other processions.[112] Consequently, in basilicas
with an eastward entrance, the faithful did not face the altar
directly but did not turn their back on it either. To do this
would indeed have been inconceivable on account of the
sacred character of the altar and of the sacrifice offered on it.
The people in the side naves needed only to change their
position slightly in order to face east; the altar would have
been more or less on their right or their left. During the
eucharistic liturgy the congregation would face the same direction as the celebrant, looking towards the open doors of
the church through which the light of the rising sun, the
symbol of the risen Christ and his Second Coming in glory,
flooded into the nave. Thus the liturgical assembly would
have formed a semicircle that opened to the east, with the
celebrating priest as its apex. The practice of priest and people facing each other arose when the profound symbolism of
facing east was no longer understood and the faithful no
longer turned eastward for the Eucharistic Prayer. This

---

[111] See, for instance, Vogel, 'L'Orientation vers l'Est', 26–29; Nußbaum,
'Die Zelebration versus populum', 155–57; and J. Lara, 'Versus Populum
Revisited', *Worship* 68 (1994): 214. With regard to the prayer *Conversi ad Dominum*, as found in Augustine's sermons, Dolbeau, *Augustin d'Hippone*, 173–75,
thinks that the faithful were facing east only for the duration of this prayer. For
the eucharistic liturgy those who stood in the nave between the altar and the
eastern entrance would turn round again and face the altar.

[112] Gamber, *Liturgie und Kirchenbau*, 23–25; cf. T. F. Mathews, 'An Early
Roman Chancel Arrangement', *RivAC* 38 (1962): 83: 'The nave is the grand
processional corridor for the hierarchy on their way to their sacred employ-
ment; the congregation area is chiefly in the aisles.'

happened especially in those basilicas where the altar was
moved from the middle of the nave to the apse.[113]

Gamber finds evidence for his hypothesis in the ancient
churches of Ravenna, the capital of the Ostrogoths, which
are closely related to the Roman and Byzantine churches of
the same date. The palace church of Theoderic the Great
(died 526), later known as S. Apollinare Nuovo, displays an
iconographic programme similar to that of later Greek
iconostases, where the enthroned Christ and the Mother of
God are depicted on the right and the left side of the 'royal
door'. In the central nave of S. Apollinare Nuovo, the right
wall shows the enthroned Christ and a group of male saints
in procession towards him; the left wall shows the Virgin
with the Child and a group of female saints in procession
towards her. Gamber takes this design to indicate that during
the celebration of the liturgy the people stood in the side
naves, with the sexes separated on either side.[114]

In Gamber's opinion Ravenna is the place of origin for
the *Ordo Romanus IV*. If this is right, *OR IV* would reflect
the episcopal liturgy celebrated in the ancient cathedral
of the city. Although this building, the Basilica Ursiana, is

---

[113] This theory is also supported by Wallraff, *Christus verus sol*, 73–74.

[114] Gamber, *Liturgie und Kirchenbau*, 79–81. The Basilica Nova of Cimitile
was also decorated with representations of saints, separated according to sex,
which would imply a separation of men and women in the church; see Paulinus of Nola, *Carmen 28*, 22–27: CSEL 30, 292. From Augustine's sermon,
preached in the cathedral-basilica of Carthage in 404 already mentioned, it is
evident that the separation of the sexes had been introduced there only a little
earlier; see Augustine, *Sermo. Dolbeau 2 (de oboedientia)*, 5: ed. Dolbeau, *Augustin d'Hippone*, 330. Cf. the observations in *Augustin d'Hippone*, 320 and 633,
with a reference to *De civitate Dei* II, 28, 5–7: CChr.SL 47, 63, where Augustine writes: 'Populi confluunt ad ecclesiam casta celebritate, honesta utriusque
sexus discretione.' However, as Duval, 'Commentaire topographique et
archéologique', 190–93, points out, archaeological evidence suggests that this
was not a universal practice in North Africa at the time of Augustine.

no longer extant in its original form, we know its ground plan. The church had four side naves and an apse in the east. The altar stood in the middle of the central nave and was walled off on all four sides by choir rails (*cancelli*). According to Gamber, *OR IV* considers the space between the altar and the apse, as well as the larger part of the nave, reserved for the clergy.[115] This area would have provided room for the schola, for the reception of the offertory gifts, for the distribution of holy communion to the faithful, and most likely for the ambo. The faithful would have stood only in the four side naves, separated by sex. This is borne out, Gamber claims, by the rubric of *OR IV* that the bishop, when receiving the gifts from the faithful, is to go from the men's side to the women's side.[116] An analogy for this peculiar arrangement can be seen in the use of the Christian East, where the faithful are at the side walls, while the central space under the dome is left free for liturgical ceremonies. Taft draws the same conclusion for churches with the altar at the entrance of the apse or in the apse and with an ambo further into the nave:

> The congregation occupied, not so much the central nave as today, but the side naves, thus leaving the center of the church

---

[115] Gamber, *Liturgie und Kirchenbau*, 134, emphasises that the instruction of *OR I*, composed for the city of Rome, 'Et tunc tolluntur cereostata de loco in quo prius steterant, ut ponantur in una linea per mediam ecclesiam' (*OR I*, 54: II, 85 Andrieu), was changed to 'et ponunt ea ante altare sicut ordinem habent' (*OR IV*, 23: II, 160 Andrieu).

[116] 'Ad partem mulieris'; *OR IV*, 41: II, 162 Andrieu. Cf. Gamber, *Liturgie und Kirchenbau*, 131–36. Apparently, the classification of 'right' and 'left' in a church—and hence also the division of the sexes—was dependent on whether the apse was directed to the east or to the west; see H. Selhorst, *Die Platzordnungen im Gläubigenraum der altchristlichen Kirche* (Münster: Aschendorff, 1931), 24–33.

free for processions and other comings and goings of the ministers demanded by the various rites.[117]

It needs to be said that there are serious objections to the hypotheses offered by Bouyer and Gamber. There is no doubt that the centre of the church was also used for liturgical ceremonies. It is questionable, however, at least in the case of large basilicas, whether the people stood during the eucharistic liturgy mainly in the side naves, which were also used for extra-liturgical functions, such as *refrigeria* and other meals. In his reconstruction of the early Lateran basilica, De Blaauw identified a long corridor (*solea*) in the nave that served the clergy for ceremonial functions, thus leaving the rest of the spacious nave free for the faithful.[118] As for Gamber's account of the liturgy in S. Apollinare Nuovo, the palace church of Theoderic, the reverential distance of the faithful to the court may well have played a role here.

Equally controversial is the view that in basilicas with an eastern entrance the whole assembly turned to the opened doors. However, our judgment in this issue should not be governed by modern sensibilities. In the context of religious practice in the ancient world, this liturgical gesture does not appear as extraordinary as it might seem today. It was the general custom in antiquity to pray towards the open sky, which meant that in a closed room one would turn to an open door or an open window for prayer. This is well attested by Jewish and Christian sources, for example, Daniel 6:10, Tobit 3:11, and Acts 10:9. The Babylonian Talmud trans-

---

[117] Taft, 'Some Notes on the Bema', 327; see also Krautheimer and Ćurčić, *Early Christian and Byzantine Architecture*, 101–2 and 217–18. Nußbaum, 'Die Zelebration versus populum', 153–54, doubts that this arrangement could be considered a common practice.

[118] De Blaauw, *Cultus et décor*, 1:127–29 and 159–60.

mits a ruling of Rabbi Hiyya bar Abba to the effect that one must not pray in a room without windows.[119] In his treatise *On Prayer*, Origen discusses the problem that arises if a house has no doors or windows facing east. He argues that one should turn towards the east, because this is a basic principle of Christian prayer, whereas turning towards the open sky is just a convention.[120] I have already referred to the archaeological evidence of Galilean synagogues from the late first century A.D. with the entrance facing towards Jerusalem. It would seem that the assembly turned towards the open doors for prayer and thus looked towards the direction of the sacred city. Against this background it would seem quite possible that for the Eucharistic Prayer the faithful, along with the priest, turned eastward towards the entrance in the east.[121]

---

[119] Babylonian Talmud, *Berakhot* 5, 1 (31a); 5, 5 (34b).

[120] Origen, *De oratione* 32: GCS Orig. II, 400–401; cf. Peterson, *Frühkirche, Judentum und Gnosis*, 1–4, and Wallraff, 'Die Ursprünge der christlichen Gebetsostung', 178–79. Cyril of Jerusalem seems to have a similar thought in mind, when he comments on the repentance of Hezekiah, who, at the point of death, 'turned his face to the wall, and prayed to the Lord' (Is 38:2): 'for thickness of walls is no hindrance to prayers sent up with devotion': *Catechesis* 2, 15: PG 33, 403A. Cyrille Vogel suggests that apsis windows were put in Christian basilicas in an attempt to reconcile turning towards the east and turning towards the open sky in prayer: Vogel, 'Croix eschatologique', 89, n. 7.

[121] The church of Tyre from the early fourth century and the Constantinian *martyrion* at the Holy Sepulchre in Jerusalem are among the few churches in the Levant that have an eastward entrance. Wilkinson, 'Orientation, Jewish and Christian', 26–29, thinks that even there the liturgical assembly prayed towards the east, that is, in the direction of the doors, which were presumably open. For a description of these two buildings, see Eusebius, *Hist. eccl.* X, 4, 37–46: GCS Euseb. II/2, 873–76, and *Vita Constantini* III, 36–39: GCS Euseb. I, 100. Alternatively, De Blaauw, *Met het oog op het licht*, 36, proposes that this type of church was meant to imitate the layout of the Jerusalem Temple, which had its entrance in the east. After Ezekiel 8:16–18, it would have been inconceivable for the congregation to turn away from the altar.

Another line of argument can be pursued if we start from the observation that facing east was accompanied by looking upward, namely towards the eastern sky which was considered the place of paradise and the scene of Christ's Second Coming.[122] As earlier indicated, the lifting up of hearts for the canon or anaphora, in response to the admonition 'Sursum corda', included the bodily gestures of standing upright, raising one's arms, and looking heavenward. It is not mere accident that the apse and triumphal arch of many basilicas were decorated with magnificent mosaics; their iconographic programmes often show close relationships with the Eucharist that is celebrated underneath.[123] The mosaics might have served to direct the attention of the liturgical assembly, whose eyes were raised up during the Eucharistic Prayer. Even the priest at the altar prayed with outstretched, raised arms (like the female figure known from the Roman catacombs as the *Orans*) and no further ritual gestures. Where the altar was placed at the entrance of the apse or in the central nave, the celebrant standing in front of it could easily have looked up towards the apse.[124] With splendid mosaics representing the celestial world, the apse may have indicated

[122] Cf. M. Righetti, *Manuale di storia liturgica*, vol. 1, *Introduzione generale*, 3d ed. (Milan: Editrice Ancora, 1964), 377–79.

[123] Cf. U. Nilgen, 'Die Bilder über dem Altar: Triumph- und Apsisbogenprogramme in Rom und Mittelitalien und ihr Bezug zur Liturgie', in *Kunst und Liturgie im Mittelalter: Akten des internationalen Kongresses der Bibliotheca Hertziana und des Nederlands Instituut te Rome, Rom, 28.–30. September 1997*, ed. N. Bock, S. de Blaauw, C. L. Frommel, and H. Kessler, *RJ*, supplement to vol. 33 (1999/2000) (Munich: Hirmer, 2000), 75–89; and C. Belting-Ihm, *Die Programme der christlichen Apsismalerei vom 4. Jahrhundert bis zur Mitte des 8. Jahrhunderts*, FKGCA 4, 2d ed. (Stuttgart: Steiner, 1992).

[124] According to Jacobsen, 'Organisationsformen des Sanktuariums', 70–71, the original layout of the Apostle's tomb in Saint Peter's, before the reordering under Gregory the Great, indicates that the priest celebrating the Eucharist stood in front of the altar, facing towards the apse, that is, westward.

the 'liturgical east' and hence the focus of prayer.[125] Needless to say, this theory is rather tentative and requires much further scrutiny. Nonetheless, it has the definite advantage that it accounts better for the correlation between liturgy, art, and architecture than the ideas of Bouyer and Gamber, which must accompany a discrepancy between the sacred rites and the space created for them.

Even if we assume that priest and people were facing one another in early Christian basilicas with an eastward entrance, we can exclude any visual contact at least for the canon, since all prayed with arms raised, looking upward. At any rate, there was not much to see on the altar, since ritual

---

[125] A case in point is the Basilica Nova of Cimitile in Campagna, built by Paulinus of Nola between 401 and 403. The new church was constructed at right angles to the old one and was aligned southward facing the highly venerated tomb of the confessor Saint Felix, with an apse in the north; see Paulinus' letter to Sulpicius Severus, *ep. 32*, 13: CSEL 29, 288. The results of the excavations on the site are summarised by D. Korol, 'Neues zur Geschichte der verehrten Gräber und des zentralen Bezirks des Pilgerheiligtums in Cimitile-Nola', *JAC* 35 (1992): 83–118. There were practical reasons for this unusual layout. Apparently, the garden north of the Basilica Vetus, built between 350 and 375 along the east-west axis, was the only free space for the new edifice. The northern apse of the Basilica Nova has two small recesses (*conchulae*), one to the right and one to the left. The description of Paulinus ('una earum immolanti hostias iubilationis antistiti patet, alia post sacerdotem capaci sinu receptat orantes') should not be taken to indicate that the bishop turned towards the east, that is, towards the right *conchula*, when he offered the eucharistic sacrifice. This interpretation is put forward by C. J. A. C. Peeters, *De liturgische dispositie van het vroegchristelijk kerkgebouw: Samenhang van cathedra, leesplaats en altaar in de basiliek van de vierde tot de zevende eeuw* (Assen: Van Gorcum, 1969), 218–19; Wilkinson, 'Orientation, Jewish and Christian', 16–17 and 22 (fig. 6); De Blaauw, *Met het oog op het licht*, 34–36; and Wallraff, *Christus verus sol*, 72–75. The new church was splendidly decorated with mosaics, including an imposing cross in the centre of the apse; cf. Belting-Ihm, *Die Programme der christlichen Apsismalerei*, 179–81. Perhaps the whole congregation, including the celebrant, was directed towards this apsidal cross, which served as the focus of prayer and so denoted the 'liturgical east' in an ideal sense.

gestures, such as signs of the cross, altar kisses, genuflections, and the elevation of the eucharistic species, were only added later.[126] Christians in the ancient world and in the early Middle Ages would not have associated real participation in the liturgy with looking at the celebrant and his actions. The *celebratio versus populum* in the modern sense was unknown to Christian antiquity,[127] and it would be anachronistic to see the eucharistic liturgy in the early Roman basilicas as its prototype.

The hypotheses that have been discussed here are no doubt preliminary and will be subject to critical examination. The Roman basilicas still raise difficult questions regarding their original layout and use. What will hold, I think, is the insight formulated by Bouyer:

> In other words, the notion that the arrangement of the Roman basilica is ideal for a Christian church because it enables priests and faithful to face each other during the celebration of Mass is really a misconstruction. It is certainly the last thing which the early Christians would have considered, and is actually contrary to the way in which the sacred functions were carried out in connection with this arrangement.[128]

Bouyer acclaims Byzantine church architecture as a genuine development of the early Christian basilica. Those elements that were not appropriate for the celebration of the liturgy were either changed or removed, so that a new type of building came into being. A major achievement was the formation of a particular iconography that stood in close connection with the sacred mysteries celebrated in the liturgy and gave

---

[126] See Bouyer, *Liturgy and Architecture*, 56–59.

[127] This point is confirmed by Nußbaum, *Der Standort des Liturgen*, 1:448.

[128] L. Bouyer, *Rite and Man: The Sense of the Sacral and Christian Liturgy*, trans. M. J. Costelloe (London: Burns and Oates, 1963), 175.

them a visible artistic form. Church architecture in the West, on the other hand, was more strongly indebted to the basilical structure. Significantly, the rich decoration of the east wall and dome in Byzantine churches has its counterpart in the Ottonian and Romanesque wall paintings and, even further developed, in the sumptuous altar compositions of the late Middle Ages, the Renaissance, and the Baroque, which display themes intimately related to the Eucharist and so give a foretaste of the eternal glory given to the faithful in the sacrifice of the Mass.[129]

Until recently, most local churches in the Latin West did not adopt the altar arrangement *versus populum* from the Roman basilicas. There was a deliberate attempt to imitate the practice of the city of Rome, which reached its climax in the self-conscious and far-ranging Carolingian programme to revive the Roman imperial idea. Some churches were modelled after Roman basilicas with a western apse, for example, Saint Gall, where the celebrant at the altar faced east towards the direction of the nave. This, however, was a relatively brief episode. Regarding liturgical orientation, the Roman church would later endorse the ceremonial use of other Western churches rather than vice versa.[130] This is also obvious from

---

[129] Cf. Bouyer, *Liturgy and Architecture*, 60–70.

[130] E. Weigand, 'Die Ostung in der frühchristlichen Architektur: Neue Tatsachen zu einer alten Problemfrage', in *Festschrift Sebastian Merkle*, ed. W. Schellberg (Düsseldorf: Schwann, 1922), 381–82, notes, with special reference to Aquileia and Ravenna, that church architecture in the Latin West cannot be confined to the city of Rome; see also Lara, 'Versus Populum Revisited', 215–16; Jacobsen, 'Organisationsformen des Sanktuariums', 76–84, and 'Altarraum und Heiligengrab als liturgisches Konzept in der Auseinandersetzung des Nordens mit Rom', in Bock et al., *Kunst und Liturgie im Mittelalter*, 65–74. Jacobsen, 'Organisationsformen des Sanktuariums', 83, states the matter clearly: 'Die "römische" Form des Sanktuariums hat im Norden trotz aller unterstützenden Versuche nur befristet Anklang gefunden; sie hat sich nicht durchgesetzt.'

the different recensions of the *Ordo Romanus I*. The earliest extant version of *OR I*, dating from the seventh century, notes that at the *Gloria* the pontiff stands at his throne, facing east (*stat versus orientem*). A more detailed version of *OR I*, dating from the first half of the eighth century, provides that at the end of the *Kyrie* the pontiff turns towards the people (*contra populum*), intones the *Gloria in excelsis Deo*, and immediately turns east again. After the *Gloria*, he turns yet again towards the faithful and greets them with the *Pax vobis*. Subsequently, he turns to the east for the *Oremus* and the following prayer.[131] The shorter, earlier recension of *OR I* was evidently composed for a Roman basilica with the entrance at the east end. When the pontiff stood at his throne, he was facing east and at the same time facing the people. The longer, later recension, on the other hand, presupposes a church with an oriented apse.[132]

---

[131] *OR I*, 51 and 53: II, 83 and 84 Andrieu.

[132] Even so, 'dirigens se pontifex contra populum incipit Gloria in excelsis Deo' need not be a Gallican addition, as Jungmann notes in the fifth, improved German edition of his standard work *Missarum Sollemnia: Eine genetische Erklärung der römischen Messe*, 5th ed. (Vienna: Herder, 1962), 1:458, n. 47. On liturgical orientation in the *Ordines Romani* of the High Middle Ages, see C. Vogel, 'Versus ad Orientem: L'Orientation dans les *Ordines romani* du haut moyen age', *StMed* 3/1 (1960): 447–69. The doctoral thesis of J. Nebel, *Die Entwicklung des römischen Meßritus im ersten Jahrtausend anhand der* Ordines Romani: *Eine synoptische Darstellung* (doctoral diss., Pontificium Athenaeum S. Anselmi de Urbe, 1998), on the development of the Roman rite of Mass in the first millennium according to the *Ordines Romani* was not available to me.

III

The Common Direction of Liturgical Prayer:
Its Theological and Spiritual Contents

1. The Relevance of Liturgical Practice in the Early Church

Even readers who find the historical part of this study convincing might ask in what sense the early Christian practice of a common direction in liturgical prayer is relevant for the life of the Church today, since times have changed. In his encyclical *Mediator Dei*, Pope Pius XII commends the study of the early liturgy, but he also warns of a misguided 'archaism':

> The liturgy of the early ages is most certainly worthy of all veneration. But ancient usage must not be esteemed more suitable and proper, either in its own right or in its significance for later times and new situations, on the simple ground that it carries the savour and aroma of antiquity.... [I]t is neither wise nor laudable to reduce everything to antiquity by every possible device.[1]

Frequent reference to the teaching and practice of the early Fathers who laid the foundation of the Christian faith is no doubt vital for the life of the Church; such a patristic *ressourcement* on its own, however, is not sufficient. John Henry

[1] Pius XII, *Littera Encyclica de Sacra Liturgia 'Mediator Dei'*, *AAS* 39 (1947): 545, nos. 61–62.

Newman and the Oxford Movement claimed that the Church of England had preserved the doctrines of the patristic Church best and thus represented the *Via Media* between the aberrations of the Church of Rome and the apostasy of Protestantism. It was Newman's great insight that recourse to this principle of 'antiquity' alone does not hold, because it cannot account for the development of Christian doctrine that took place already in the apostolic age and continued through the Middle Ages until the present day, being authenticated by the infallible Magisterium of the Catholic Church. Divine revelation was communicated to the world once for all by inspired teachers. Nonetheless, it was received and transmitted by human agents; therefore it needed time and thought for its complete elucidation. Newman realised that it is inconsistent to acknowledge the Church Fathers as authorities in matters of revealed truth, while at the same time rejecting the tradition of the medieval Church. He says pointedly: 'The *Via Media* has slept in libraries; it is a substitute of infancy for manhood.'[2] This obtains not only for the doctrine of the faith but also for the Church's liturgy.[3] Newman illustrates his point with a telling image:

[2] J. H. Newman, *Apologia pro Vita Sua* (London: Longman, Green, Longman, Roberts and Green, 1864), 204.

[3] Newman, *An Essay on the Development of Christian Doctrine*, new ed. (London: Basil Montagu Pickering, 1878), 29–30. 'The increase and expansion of the Christian Creed and Ritual, and the variations which have attended the process in the case of individual writers and Churches, are the necessary attendants on any philosophy or polity which takes possession of the intellect and heart, and has had any wide or extended dominion; that, from the nature of the human mind, time is necessary for the full comprehension and perfection of great ideas; and that the highest and most wonderful truths, though communicated to the world once for all by inspired teachers, could not be comprehended all at once by the recipients, but, as being received and transmitted by minds not inspired and media which were human, have required

It is indeed sometimes said that the stream is clearest near the spring. Whatever use may fairly be made of this image, it does not apply to the history of a philosophy or belief, which on the contrary is more equable, and purer, and stronger, when its bed has become deep, and broad, and full.[4]

Newman's crucial insight seems to resonate in Ratzinger's early criticism of the liturgical reform:

Its theological origin has infected the liturgical movement with what I will call a certain archaism, which has for its purpose the restoration of the Roman liturgy in its classical form before it became overlaid by medieval and Carolingian accretions. This view would set up as the criterion of liturgical renewal not the question: How should it be? but rather the question: How was it at that time? To which we can only say that whereas to know how things were at that time is of invaluable help to us in coping with the problems of our own time, it cannot be simply the standard by which reform is measured. It is very important and helpful, for instance, to know how things were done under Gregory the Great, but that is no reason at all why they should be done in the very same way today. This archaism has often made us close our eyes to the good things which have been evolved in later developments and has caused us to set the taste of one period up on a pedestal; admittedly, it was a splendid period which rightly commands the greatest respect and affection, but its taste can no more be made a matter of absolute dogma than the taste of any other period.[5]

---

only the longer time and deeper thought for their full elucidation. This may be called the *Theory of Development of Doctrine*.'

[4] Ibid., 40.

[5] J. Ratzinger, 'Catholicism after the Council', trans. P. Russell, *The Furrow* 18 (1967): 10.

Ratzinger's perceptive analysis exposes the curious ambivalence of a liturgical purism that oscillates between a tendency towards archaism and an uncontrolled urge for novelty:

> But as well as going back to the ancient liturgy, we can have the very opposite thing too, and that brings us to the other root from which the liturgical revival has sprung. Many will remember a time, not very many years ago, when the Gregorian chant was extolled as the only legitimate form of Church music, and against this there was no appeal. The orchestra was driven out of the church with a flaming sword—it was bad enough having Carolingian elements in the ancient Roman liturgy, but these orchestral Masses dating only from the Baroque age. After all! Now we see how the recent upsurge of enthusiasm for jazz music has opened the doors of the church to orchestras of vastly different style to those older orchestras, and it makes us wonder somehow whether we can give serious credence any more to all those things which claim to be an expression of liturgical renewal. Mere archaism does not help matters along but neither does mere modernisation.[6]

Almost twenty years later in the famous *Ratzinger Report*, the Prefect of the Congregation for the Doctrine of the Faith reiterated this critique, adding that in the Middle Ages and, in many respects, in the age of the Baroque, the liturgy developed depth and maturity that cannot easily be disregarded.[7]

A striking example of such archaism is the suggestion that the priest should face the people for the celebration of the Eucharist because this was the position of Jesus vis-à-vis the

---

[6] Ibid., 11.

[7] J. Ratzinger, with V. Messori, *The Ratzinger Report: An Exclusive Interview on the State of the Church*, trans. S. Attanasio and G. Harrison (San Francisco: Ignatius Press, 1985), 131–32; see now also J. Ratzinger, *The Spirit of the Liturgy*, trans. J. Saward (San Francisco: Ignatius Press, 2000), 81–82 and 85–91.

apostles at the Last Supper. There are two fundamental flaws in this idea. First, it is tacitly assumed that the ritual shape of the Eucharist is, or at any rate should be, a reproduction of the Upper Room where the Last Supper was held. The sacrament of the New Covenant was instituted in the context of a Jewish festal meal, but it was the new reality, not the meal as such, that Christ commanded us to repeat in memory of him. The eucharistic sacrifice of Our Lord's Body and Blood perpetuates the saving sacrifice of the Cross until he comes again in glory. Christian worship refers to the paschal mystery, that is, the total reality of Christ's Passion, death, and Resurrection, and cannot be reduced to the category of a 'meal'. Hence it was appropriate that, in earliest times, this new reality was distinguished from its Jewish context and developed its own ritual shape. It would be a most deceptive archaism to think that the transition from a Jewish meal celebration to an act of liturgical worship 'before the Lord' (cf. Deut 26:10 and elsewhere) could be or even should be reversed.[8]

The second flaw in this suggestion is a mistaken view of the circumstances at the Last Supper itself. As has already been said, it was customary for the diners to recline on couches arranged in a semicircle, with small tables being used for holding food and dishes. The place of honour was on the right of the semicircle. From about the thirteenth century, depictions of the Last Supper adopted the contemporary seating arrangement, with Jesus occupying the place of honour in the middle of a large table and the apostles to his right and

---

[8] Cf. Ratzinger, *Spirit of the Liturgy*, 79: 'This new and all-encompassing form of worship could not be derived simply from the meal but had to be defined through the interconnection of Temple and synagogue, Word and sacrament, cosmos and history'; see also J. A. Jungmann, 'Der neue Altar', *Der Seelsorger* 37 (1967): 375.

left, as, for example, in Leonardo da Vinci's famous fresco in Milan. An image of this type may well have been in the mind of Martin Luther when, in 1526, he suggested that the altar should not remain in its old position and that the priest should always face the people, as no doubt Christ did at the Last Supper.[9] In a number of churches the Reformers modified the existing medieval altar with a retable so that the celebrant could stand behind it, facing the people. The ceremonial for which this sanctuary arrangement provided would seem to reflect Luther's novel understanding of the institution narrative. In acrimonious polemics, Luther condemned the Roman Canon as idolatrous, and for liturgical purposes he reduced it to the words of consecration that were to be understood as proclamation of the Word of God and hence to be chanted in the Gospel tone.[10] Still, Luther's proposal that the *verba consecrationis* should be said, or rather sung, facing the people was scarcely put into practice in the sixteenth century. It was taken up by the Reformed in southwest Germany (for example by Martin Bucer in Straßburg, where free-standing tables for the celebration of the Lord's Supper were introduced) but never in Wittenberg.[11] Until recently, most Lutheran churches retained the common direction of

[9] However, Luther did not insist on this point: 'Nu, das erharre seyner zeyt'; *Deutsche Messe und Ordnung Gottesdiensts*, 'Des Sonntags für die Laien': Weimarer Ausgabe XIX, 80. For an English translation, see B.J. Kidd, *Documents Illustrative of the Continental Reformation* (Oxford: Clarendon Press, 1911), 199.

[10] Cf. H.B. Meyer, *Luther und die Messe: Eine liturgiewissenschaftliche Untersuchung über das Verhältnis Luthers zum Meßwesen des späten Mittelalters*, KKTS 11 (Paderborn: Bonifacius-Druckerei, 1965), 246–61, esp. 256–57, and J.A. Jungmann, *Messe im Gottesvolk: Ein nachkonziliarer Durchblick durch Missarum Sollemnia* (Freiburg: Herder, 1970), 21.

[11] Cf. Meyer, *Luther und die Messe*, 259–60, and F. Schulz, 'Das Mahl der Brüder: Herrenmahl in neuer Gestalt', *JLH* 15 (1970): 34.

liturgical prayer, even though they rejected the sacrificial understanding of the Mass. In fact, rising demands for celebration of Holy Communion facing the people since Vatican II have met with the opposition of Protestant theologians and have not been implemented much.[12]

True, cosmological orientation and its attendant eschatological symbolism have gradually been lost in the Latin Church.[13] From the sixteenth century, at the latest, it was no longer the general custom in the West to align churches and altars along the east–west axis.[14] This is exemplified in Ludwig Ciconiolanus' *Directorium divinorum officiorum iuxta Romanae curiae ritum*, which was approved by Pope Paul III in 1539. Ciconiolanus discusses the question (which had been raised some time earlier) as to whether one can put up an altar facing west. Where this was done, it used to be customary, he explains, for the priest to stand on the far side of the altar and celebrate Mass '*versa facie ad populum*', but according to the decision of the popes and the universal practice of the Church, the priest now celebrates Mass 'with his back to the people (*ad populum versis tergis*)'. There is no binding law that an altar cannot be constructed facing west; one is free to put the altar facing any of the cardinal points.[15]

---

[12] Cf. V. Walther, ' "Celebratio versus populum": Evangelisches Echo und Fragen an den evangelischen Gottesdienst', *HlD* 53 (1999): 137–42, with further references.

[13] This is rightly said by the Congregation for Divine Worship in its 'Editoriale: Pregare "ad orientem versus"', *Not* 29 (1993): 247.

[14] This development also led to misconceptions about early Roman church architecture, as documented by S. de Blaauw, *Met het oog op het licht: Een vergeten principe in de oriëntatie van het vroegchristelijk kerkgebouw*, Nijmeegse Kunsthistorische Cahiers 2 (Nijmegen: Nijmegen University Press, 2000), 43–51.

[15] Ciconiolanus, *Directorium divinorum officiorum*, ed. J. W. Legg, *Tracts on the Mass*, HBS 27 (London: Harrison, 1904), 202; cf. O. Nußbaum, 'Die Zelebration versus populum und der Opfercharakter der Messe', *ZKTh* 93 (1971): 161. The phrase 'cum aliter a summis Pontificibus constitutum sit' might refer

That the Christian direction of prayer had not yet fallen into oblivion is shown by Saint Charles Borromeo's *Instructiones fabricae et supellectilis ecclesiasticae* of 1577, a key work on the renewal of church architecture after the Council of Trent. The archbishop of Milan says that the *capella major* must be oriented, with the main altar facing east. Where this is impossible, it can be directed towards another cardinal point (except north), but preferably towards the west, 'as, in accordance with the rite of the Church (*pro Ritu Ecclesiae*), the sacrifice of the Mass is celebrated at the main altar by the priest with his face turned towards the people'.[16] Borromeo

---

to a decree of Pope Vigilius (537–555), which is also mentioned by Durandus, *Rationale divinorum officiorum* V, II, 57: CChr.CM 140A, 42. This decree, however, is not found among the extant writings of Vigilius, as already noted by F. J. Dölger, *Sol salutis: Gebet und Gesang im christlichen Altertum: Mit besonderer Rücksicht auf die Ostung in Gebet und Liturgie*, 2d ed., LF 4/5 (Münster: Aschendorff, 1925), 333–34. Walafrid Strabo writes around 830 that altars can be erected towards the west and towards other cardinal points, but at the same time he gives clear evidence that the eastward direction of prayer almost always determined the construction of churches: 'Sed tamen usus frequentior ... et rationi vicinior habet in orientem orantes converti et pluralitatem maximam ecclesiarum eo tenore constitui'; Walafrid Strabo, *Libellus de exordiis et incrementis quarundam in observationibus ecclesiasticis rerum*, 4: ed. A. Boretius and V. Krause (MGH.Cap 2), 478.22–24, cf. 477–78. See also W. Jacobsen, 'Organisationsformen des Sanktuariums im spätantiken und mittelalterlichen Kirchenbau: Wechselwirkungen von Altarraum und Liturgie aus kunsthistorischer Perspektive', in *Kölnische Liturgie und ihre Geschichte: Studien zur interdisziplinären Erforschung des Gottesdienstes im Erzbistum Köln*, ed. A. Gerhards and A. Odenthal, LWQF 87 (Münster: Aschendorff, 2000), 81.

[16] C. Borromeo, *Instructiones fabricae et supellectilis ecclesiasticae, Lib. I. Cap. X, De cappella maiori*, ed. S. della Torre and M. Marinelli, trans. M. Marinelli, Monumenta studia instrumenta liturgica 8 (Vatican City: Libreria Editrice Vaticana, 2000); trans. E. C. Voelker, *Charles Borromeo's* Instructiones Fabricae et Supellectilis Ecclesiasticae, *1577: A Translation with Commentary and Analysis* (Ph.D. diss., Syracuse University, 1977), 124 (modified). The phrase 'pro Ritu Ecclesiae' is an example of 'the rather terse directives found in the text', which are noted by Voelker, *Charles Borromeo's* Instructiones, 5.

must have had in mind those Roman basilicas with a westward apse and an eastward entrance, where Mass was celebrated facing the people; this practice was no doubt familiar
to him. The archbishop's efforts to renew and regulate church
architecture were part of a comprehensive programme to reclaim Milan's title of *Secunda Roma*.[17] Still, for Borromeo
the eastward direction was the paramount principle for liturgy and church architecture.[18]

Given the historical development in the West since the
end of the Middle Ages, the *Notitiae* editoral already referred
to concludes that facing east in prayer is not an inviolable
element and cannot be considered a fundamental principle
of the Christian liturgical tradition. Moreover, with reference to the encyclical *Mediator Dei* of Pope Pius XII, the
question is raised whether it would not be archaeologising
to see in the arrangement of the altar towards the east the
decisive key to a correct celebration of the Eucharist.[19] The
response to this question might be in the affirmative, if it
were only a matter of directing the altar towards one of the
cardinal points. For the Christians of the first millennium or
so, the east had a very distincive theological and liturgical
significance: facing east in prayer embodied their lively hope
for the Second Coming of the risen and ascended Christ in
glory, to judge the living and the dead; it also symbolised the
journey of the pilgrim people of God towards the future

[17] Cf. the study of S. Mayer-Himmelheber, *Bischöfliche Kunstpolitik nach dem
Tridentinum: Der Secunda-Roma-Anspruch Carlo Borromeos und die mailändischen
Verordnungen zu Bau und Ausstattung von Kirchen* (Munich: Tuduv-
Verlagsgesellschaft, 1984).

[18] Hence the comments of P. M. Gy, '*L'Esprit de la liturgie* du Cardinal Ratzinger est-il fidèle au Concile, ou en réaction contre?' *La Maison-Dieu* 229
(2002): 174, are misleading.

[19] Congregatio de Cultu Divino et Disciplina Sacramentorum, 'Editoriale',
247.

bliss promised to them, a foretaste of which was made present in the celebration of the eucharistic sacrifice. But this eschatological expectation was severed from its cosmological context, and it can be argued that the attempt to restore this connection would be just another archaism—one indeed of as equally doubtful merit as the many others that have been tried in the last few decades. However, what is at issue here is the common direction of priest and people in liturgical prayer. This is not a form of archaism, if only because it was the virtually universal practice in the Latin Church until the most recent times and is part of the liturgical heritage in the Churches of the Byzantine, Syriac, Armenian, Coptic, and Ethiopian traditions. It is still the custom in most of the Eastern rites for priest and people to face the same direction in prayer, at least during the anaphora. That a few Eastern Catholic Churches, for example, the Maronite and the Syro-Malabar, have lately adopted the *celebratio versus populum* is owing to modern Latin influence and not in keeping with their authentic traditions. For this reason, the Congregation for the Oriental Churches declared in its instruction *Il Padre incomprensibile* of 6 January 1996 that the ancient tradition of praying towards the east has a profound liturgical and spiritual value and must be preserved in the Eastern rites.[20]

The orientation of the celebrant during the eucharistic liturgy is a thorny question in the Syro-Malabar Church of India, which is the second largest Eastern Catholic Church, counting almost four million faithful, and which was raised to the status of a Major Archepiscopal Church *sui iuris* by

---

[20] Congregatio pro Ecclesiis Orientalibus, *Instruzione per l'applicazione delle prescrizioni liturgiche del Codice dei Canoni delle Chiese Orientali 'Il Padre incomprensibile'* (Vatican City: Libreria Editrice Vaticana, 1996), 85–86, no. 107; this instruction can also be found in E. Lora, ed., *Enchiridion Vaticanum 15: Documenti ufficiali della Santa Sede 1996* (Bologna: Dehoniane, 1999), 88–89.

Pope John Paul II in 1992. After the Second Vatican Council, Mass facing the people was introduced among the Syro-Malabar as a spontaneous practice and without approval from the authorities. In fact, the eastward direction is of particular significance in the East Syrian liturgical tradition, to which the Syro-Malabar rite belongs. So the introduction of the *celebratio versus populum* cannot be captured with the catchword inculturation but, rather, indicates a crisis of identity. Far from being a contribution towards Indianisation, it furthers the Latinisation of the Syro-Malabar rite, which has had a tormented history since the sixteenth century. Restoring the celebrant's position *versus orientem*, at least for the anaphora, is accordingly part of the joint effort of the Syro-Malabar bishops and the Holy See to revive the genuine East Syrian traditions of this Church.[21]

In the course of this study, it has been shown that facing east in the Eucharist has had a profound significance in the Christian tradition. At the same time, the intrinsic meaning of this liturgical gesture transcends the mere turning towards one of the cardinal points. In fact, 'liturgical orientation' in an ideal sense can even be disconnected from its strict geographical context. What is at stake here is the common direction of priest and people in liturgical prayer.[22] Drawing

[21] Cf. P. Vazheeparampil, *The Making and Unmaking of Tradition: Towards a Theology of the Liturgical Renewal in the Syro-Malabar Church* (Rome: Mar Thoma Yogam, 1998), esp. 248–52, on facing east in the liturgy, and P. Pallath, ed., *La liturgia eucaristica della chiesa siro-malabarese*, Quaderni di Rivista Liturgica 1 (Padua: Edizioni Messagero, 2000), 125–27.

[22] J. A. Jungmann, *The Mass of the Roman Rite: Its Origins and Development (Missarum Sollemnia)*, trans. F. A. Brunner, vol. 1 (New York: Benziger Brothers, 1951), 255, n. 15: 'Orientation at prayer and the symbolism it entails has lost much of its meaning for us. But the basic principle that at prayer all—including even the celebrant—should take a God-ward stance, could easily be at work here too, in establishing the celebrant's position at the altar. If Mass

on contemporary theologians, I shall now present the theological and spiritual implications of this traditional practice.

2. Turning to the Lord—The Theological Dimension of Liturgical Practice

a. The cosmic symbolism of sacramental worship

Taking up the suggestion of Jungmann, Cardinal Ratzinger emphasises that the ancient practice of priest and people facing the same way expresses the nature of the Eucharist as a common act of trinitarian worship. The whole assembly is united in facing eastward, that is, in turning to the Lord, as is conveyed in Augustine's prayer after the sermon, *Conversi ad Dominum*. Ratzinger considers it momentous that this cosmic symbolism was incorporated into the community celebration. By means of a liturgical gesture, the true location and the true context of the Eucharist are opened up, namely, the whole cosmos. The cosmic sign of the sun rising from the east has been interpreted in two ways: first, as a sign of the risen Christ and thus also of the Father's power and the working of the Holy Spirit; second, as a sign of hope in the Parousia. The common orientation in liturgical prayer thus not only conveys the trinitarian dimension of the Eucharist but also witnesses to a theology of hope in Christ's

---

were only a service of instruction or a Communion celebration, the other position, facing the people, would be more natural. But it is different if the Mass is an immolation and homage to God.' Similarly, K. Gamber, *Liturgie und Kirchenbau: Studien zur Geschichte der Meßfeier und des Gotteshauses in der Frühzeit*, SPLi 6 (Regensburg: Pustet, 1976), 26–27.

Second Coming. It realizes the Christian synthesis of cosmos and history.[23]

The cosmic symbolism of sacramental worship allows the world to remain transparent for transcendent reality. The orientation of prayer reaches beyond the visible altar towards eschatological fulfilment, which is anticipated in the celebration of the Eucharist. The priest facing the same direction as the faithful when he stands at the altar leads the people of God on their way towards meeting the Lord who is to come again. This movement towards the Lord, who is 'the rising sun of history',[24] has found its sublime artistic expression in the sanctuaries of the first millennium, where representations of the Cross or of the glorified Christ mark the goal of the assembly's earthly pilgrimage. The eschatological character of the Eucharist is kept alive by this looking out for the Lord; we are reminded that the celebration of the sacrament is a participation in the heavenly liturgy and a pledge of future glory in the presence of the living God. This trinitarian dynamism gives the Eucharist its greatness, saves the individual community from closing into itself, and opens it towards the assembly of the saints in the heavenly city, as envisaged in the Letter to the Hebrews:

[23] J. Ratzinger, *The Feast of Faith: Approaches to a Theology of the Liturgy*, trans. G. Harrison (San Francisco: Ignatius Press, 1986), 140–41. This point is also made by the Roman Congregation for Divine Worship: 'The arrangement of the altar in such a way that the celebrant and the faithful face east . . . is a splendid application of the "parousial" character of the Eucharist. The mystery of Christ is celebrated *donec veniat de caelis*', translating 'Editoriale', 246. See now Ratzinger, *Spirit of the Liturgy*, 24–34 and 62–84, and, for an in-depth review of Ratzinger's book *The Spirit of the Liturgy*, P. Cantoni, 'Per un "nuovo" movimento liturgico', *Cristianità* 30 (2002): 5–18.

[24] Ratzinger, *Spirit of the Liturgy*, 84; see also L. Bouyer, *Liturgy and Architecture* (Notre Dame, Ind.: University of Notre Dame Press, 1967), 95–96.

> But you have come to Mount Zion and to the city of the
> living God, the heavenly Jerusalem, and to innumerable an-
> gels in festal gathering, and to the assembly of the first-born
> who are enrolled in heaven, and to a judge who is God of
> all, and to the spirits of just men made perfect, and to Jesus,
> the mediator of a new covenant, and to the sprinkled blood
> that speaks more graciously than the blood of Abel (Heb
> 12:22–24).

Cardinal Christoph Schönborn develops this line of reason-
ing by adding the thought that the whole liturgy is celebrated *obviam Sponso*, facing the Bridegroom. The faithful
so anticipate the Lord's Second Coming and can be likened
to the virgins in the Gospel parable: 'But at midnight there
was a cry, "Behold, the bridegroom! Come out to meet him" '
(Mt 25:6). Schönborn emphasises that signs and gestures, such
as the common direction of liturgical prayer, are vital for
'incarnating' the faith.[25]

By contrast, the constant face-to-face position of priest
and people expresses a symbolism of its own and suggests a
closed circle. The ideal of the Christian church is not a cir-
cular building with altar, ambo, and sedilia in the centre. It is
not mere accident that samples of this type are hardly found
before the second half of the twentieth century; the *celebratio
versus populum* tends to diminish the transcendent dimension
of the Eucharist to such an extent that it generates the no-
tion of a closed society. The communal character of the liturgy is no doubt important, but it is only one aspect of the
liturgy. The danger is that the congregation can become com-
placent and entertain a misconceived autonomy, thus dis-

---

[25] Cf. C. Schönborn, *Loving the Church: Spiritual Exercises Preached in the Presence of Pope John Paul II*, trans. J. Saward (San Francisco: Ignatius Press, 1998), 203–6.

connecting itself from the other assemblies of the faithful and from the invisible assembly of the saints in heaven, so that the community would just be in dialogue with itself.[26] This betrays not only a deficient ecclesiology but also an erroneous concept of God. The eclipse of transcendence is a powerful current of the *Zeitgeist* that must not be underestimated. Half a century ago, Henri de Lubac warned Christians to be on guard 'against the present tendency to absorb God into the human community'.[27] Today, we are threatened by what Aidan Nichols calls 'cultic immanentism', 'the danger . . . of a congregation's covert self-reference in a horizontal, humanistic world'.[28]

This argument is corroborated by the keen analysis of the Protestant sociologist of religion Peter L. Berger:

> This new position makes wonderfully clear that the sacred being that is worshiped exists not *outside* the gathered community but rather *inside* it. It is a powerful symbolic reversal.[29]

Berger certainly does not intend to deny the communal character of Christian worship. What he does object to is a community worshiping itself, which he censures, from a biblical point of view, as a form of idolatry. The recent liturgical changes have laid an emphasis on a gathering of people enjoying the experience of community, and this in turn conveys the impression that nothing extraordinary is happening:

[26] Cf. Ratzinger, *The Feast of Faith*, 142–43, and J. A. Jungmann, review of O. Nußbaum, *Der Standort des Liturgen am christlichen Altar vor dem Jahre 1000*, *ZKTh* 88 (1966): 449.

[27] H. de Lubac, *The Splendor of the Church*, trans. M. Mason (San Francisco: Ignatius Press, 1999), 226.

[28] A. Nichols, *Looking at the Liturgy: A Critical View of Its Contemporary Form* (San Francisco: Ignatius Press, 1996), 97.

[29] P. L. Berger, *A Far Glory: The Quest for Faith in an Age of Credulity* (New York: Free Press, 1992), 95.

It seems to me that all of this reflects a serious mistake about the nature of worship. All true worship is a difficult attempt to reach out for transcendence. It is this reaching *out* that must be symbolized, by whatever resources a particular tradition has at hand. The chosen form will certainly have a communal aspect. But the community itself is not the object of the exercise; at best it is the subject.[30]

For Berger, as for Ratzinger, the common direction of prayer stands for the trinitarian and eschatological dynamism of the Christian liturgy.[31]

An equally critical note is struck by Tena Garriga in the survey of liturgical life in the Catholic Church that he presented at a symposium about the reception of the Second Vatican Council held in the Vatican on the occasion of the Great Jubilee 2000. Garriga perceives a widespread desacra-

---

[30] And Berger continues: 'I further think that in the Christian case, the religious community is what Wolfhart Pannenberg has called "proleptic": The congregation itself is not what matters, but the community of the Kingdom of God which the gathered congregation feebly foreshadows. Nor is this proleptic community contained within the walls of a particular sanctuary: It includes the community of the living everywhere, and of the living and the dead; ultimately it includes the worshiping community of the angels and all creation': ibid., 96–97.

[31] For similar criticism, see J. Macquarrie, 'Subjectivity and Objectivity in Theology and Worship', *Worship* 41 (1967): 158; C. Napier, 'The Altar in the Contemporary Church', *CleR* 57 (1972): 629; W. Siebel, *Liturgie als Angebot: Bemerkungen aus soziologischer Sicht* (Berlin: Morus-Verlag, 1972), 16–21; H. U. von Balthasar, 'Die Würde der Liturgie', *IkaZ* 7 (1978): 481–87; and, most recently, B. Harbert, 'Paradise and the Liturgy', *NBl* 83 (2002): 30–41. The Lithuanian theologian Benas Ulevičius argues in his study *The Divine East: The Post-Vatican Liturgical Reform and the Question of 'Turning the Altars'* that where the liturgical heritage of the Church is no longer esteemed and preserved, especially regarding the traditional orientation of the altars, the disenchanted people will literally turn to the 'divine east' (*dieviškieji rytai*), that is, to Eastern religions, with their spiritual aspirations. See B. Ulevičius, *Dieviškieji Rytai: Povatikaninė liturginė reforma ir 'altorių atgręžimo' klausimas* (Vilnius: Aidai, 2002).

lisation and secularisation of the liturgy, which go with a purely horizontal vision of Christian life and have their roots in a deficient Christology.[32]

Paradoxically, efforts to give the liturgy a more 'communal' character make it more centred on the celebrating priest. Hans Urs von Balthasar addresses the peculiar correlation between liturgical cosiness (*Gemütlichkeit*) and this new variety of clericalism.

> An element lacking in good taste has crept into the liturgy since the (falsely interpreted) Council, namely, the joviality and familiarity of the celebrant with the congregation. People come, however, for prayer and not for a cozy encounter. Oddly enough, because of this misinterpretation, one gets the impression that the post-conciliar liturgy has become more clerical than it was in the days when the priest functioned as mere servant of the mystery being celebrated. Before and after the liturgy, personal contact is entirely in place, but during the celebration everyone's attention should be directed to the one Lord.[33]

[32] T. Garriga, 'La sacra liturgia fonte e culmina della vita ecclesiale', in *Il Concilio Vaticano II: Recezione e attualità alla luce del Giubileo*, ed. R. Fisichella (Milan: San Paolo, 2000), 51–54; see also 59–60, where he points out that intelligibility is not an absolute principle in the liturgy: 'Ora: è assolutamente certo che tutto deve essere fatto in vista della comprensione? E ancora, di quale comprensione? Intellettuale, vitale? L'ingresso nella liturgia non si attua mediante grandi spiegazioni, ma applicando il grande principio di san Benedetto, citato dalla *Sacrosanctum Concilium: Mens nostra concordet voci nostrae*. La liturgia ha una *vox* che si deve lasciare udire nitidamente: la *vox* della liturgia sono le parole e le cose, i gesti, i silenzi della preghiera della Chiesa.'

[33] Balthasar, 'Die Würde der Liturgie', 134. See also the pungent analysis of the German sociologist and psychoanalyst Alfred Lorenzer, who regards himself, not as part of the ongoing debate within the Church, but as an external observer: 'Nichts vom Tun und Lassen der Zelebranten bleibt dem Zuschauer verborgen. Ausdrücklich im Gegensatz zur ostkirchlichen Diskretion, die das sakrale Handeln verbirgt, überrundet die neue Liturgie selbst die reformatorische Nüchternheit durch Veralltäglichung des Sakramentalen. . . . Seines

What about the current idea that the actions of the celebrant should be made visible to the congregation and hence require the arrangement of the altar towards the people? It may perhaps be argued that this forms part of the faith's being 'incarnated', that is, taking shape in the liturgy. As we have already seen, the visibility of the priest's actions at the altar was of hardly any interest to Christians in the first millennium; looking at the celebrant was not considered a requirement for real participation in liturgical prayer. The important principle was not one of visibility but of audibility. This is made clear by Michael Napier:

> The notion that the congregation at Mass are in some sense spectators of what takes place is an unfortunate hangover from a period when they had no other choice. If it survives in the new liturgy it means that the whole purpose of liturgical reform has not been understood, and nothing is more likely to help it survive than an arrangement which focuses attention on the priest's actions at the altar.[34]

---

gestischen Schmuckes beraubt, aber als instrumenteller Handlungskomplex umständlich bewahrt und nun vor aller Augen vorgeführt in jener Scheindurchsichtigkeit, die die Sinnlichkeit des Hantierens mit der Durchsichtigkeit des Mythos verwechselt, vorgeführt in einer Anordnung jedenfalls, in der jedes Detail dieses Eßrituals aufdringlich exhibiert wird': A. Lorenzer, *Das Konzil der Buchhalter: Die Zerstörung der Sinnlichkeit: Eine Religionskritik*, unabridged ed. (Frankfurt am Main: Fischer-Taschenbuch-Verlag, 1984), 192. Lorenzer's thought-provoking critique is resumed from the perspective of postmodernist authors, such as Foucault and Derrida, by J. Hoff, 'Das Verschwinden des Körpers: Eine Kritik an der "Wut des Verstehens" in der Liturgie', *HerKor* 54 (2000): 154.

[34] Napier, 'The Altar in the Contemporary Church', 628–29; cf. Jungmann, 'Der neue Altar', 379; and Ratzinger, *Spirit of the Liturgy*, 81: 'Looking at the priest has no importance. What matters is looking together at the Lord. It is not now a question of dialogue, but of common worship, of setting off toward the One who is to come. What corresponds with the reality of what is happening is not the closed circle but the common movement forward, ex-

As Napier points out, the common direction of prayer is in keeping with the intention of the liturgical reform, which has restored the priority of audibility over visibility. Consequently, the actions of the priest have been greatly reduced in the rubrics of the *Novus Ordo Missae*.

It is argued in favour of the celebration facing the people that it is indispensable for the dialogue between celebrant and congregation. The *versus populum* position no doubt makes sense for those parts of the Mass where priest and people are in dialogue, especially the Liturgy of the Word. But the paramount principle of Christian worship is the dialogue between the people of God as a whole (including the celebrant) and God, to whom their prayer is addressed. If this principle is not manifest in the shape of the liturgy, the Eucharist gives the appearance of nothing more than a catechetical instruction.[35] The synagogue service, one of the roots of Christian worship, was not purely didactic; rather, it had a ritual, indeed a sacramental dimension, which was shown in turning for prayer towards the Torah shrine and thus to the Holy of Holies in the Temple. This sacramental dimension is even more definite in the liturgy of the New Covenant. The face-to-face position of priest and people is fitting for catechesis but not for the celebration of the Eucharist.

---

pressed in a common direction for prayer.' Interestingly, Paul Claudel, a few weeks before his death in 1955, spoke in strong terms against the celebration of Mass *versus populum*. As the French writer observed, the priest, when facing the people, speaks 'into the void', with the faithful as 'curious spectators': Paul Claudel, 'La Messe à l'envers', *Figaro littéraire* of 29 January 1955, quoted in J. A. Jungmann, *Liturgisches Erbe und pastorale Gegenwart: Studien und Vorträge* (Innsbruck: Tyrolia, 1960), 126.

[35] Cf. M. Kunzler, 'La liturgia all'inizio del Terzo Millennio', in *Il Concilio Vaticano II: Recezione e attualità alla luce del Giubileo*, ed. R. Fisichella (Milan: San Paolo, 2000), 224–27, who criticises the erroneous tendency to reduce worship to pedagogy.

Metzger goes so far as to maintain that the *celebratio versus populum* does not show the true aspect of the Church and of her ministry.[36] The phrases 'facing the people' and 'back to the people' exclude the one to whom all prayer is directed, namely, God. The priest does not celebrate the Eucharist 'facing the people'; rather, the whole congregation celebrates facing God, through Jesus Christ in the Holy Spirit. This dialogue between God and his whole people is represented most appropriately in the celebration *versus orientem* or *versus absidem*. On a principal note, Metzger comments that man is bound to space and time, and so is his prayer to God. When we invoke God, our prayer needs to be incarnated, as it were. We cannot leave behind completely these spatial and temporal representations of God, but we must always endeavour to purify them. The common direction of prayer towards the east is the supreme purification of this spatial representation of God.[37] A similar argument is already found in Augustine's commentary on the first petition of the Lord's Prayer.[38] The common direction of priest and people in prayer, which is not absolutely bound towards one of the cardinal points, manifests a God-ward stance and so reveals the true nature of the Church.

[36] M. Metzger, 'La Place des liturges à l'autel', *RevSR* 45 (1971): 140: 'Le grand reproche que l'on peut formuler contre la célébration "face au peuple" est qu'une telle manière de faire n'exprime pas le vrai visage de l'Église et du ministère.'

[37] See ibid., 140–41. The question is well put by A. Stock, 'Gotteshaus und Kirchgang', *LJ* 39 (1989): 8: 'Der sakrale Raum, wie immer man ihn konzipiert, transformiert die theologische in eine theotopische Frage, die sich auf den schlichten Kehrvers bringen läßt: "Wohin soll ich mich wenden und wie begegnen dir?" Wohin also wenden wir uns, wenn wir uns in unseren heutigen Kirchenräumen zu Gott wenden wollen?'

[38] Augustine, *De sermone domini in monte* II, 5, 17–18: CChr.SL 35, 107–9. Cf. also Ratzinger, *Spirit of the Liturgy*, 75–76.

The import of the ecclesiological aspects emphasised by Metzger, as well as the eschatological and trinitarian dimension of the eucharistic liturgy brought to the fore by Ratzinger, have been confirmed by the Roman Congregation for Divine Worship. In the Mass, the Second Coming of the Lord in glory is anticipated sacramentally. When she celebrates the sacrament of her redemption the Church is necessarily oriented towards the Lord; in communion with him and through his mediation, she addresses her prayers and offerings to the Father, in the unity of the Holy Spirit. The arrangement of the altar in such a way that the celebrant and the faithful face eastward brings to light the 'parousial' character of Eucharist, for the mystery of Christ is being celebrated *donec veniat in caelis*. It is only during the dialogue parts of the Mass that the priest addresses himself to the people. Apart from this, he prays to the Father through Christ in the Holy Spirit. [39]

b. The position of the celebrant and the sacrificial character of the Mass

It would seem that the common direction in liturgical prayer is closely linked to the understanding of the Mass as a sacrifice. In his critical review of Nußbaum's study, Jungmann observes that patristic evidence for the eastward position of the celebrant is strongest where the sacrificial understanding of the Eucharist was clearly developed at an early stage, particularly in Syria. He notes that this connection is not accidental. Rather, the basic principle that the celebrant at the altar should take a God-ward stance at prayer and face the

---

[39] Congregatio de Cultu Divino et Disciplina Sacramentorum, 'Editoriale', 245–46.

same way as the people expresses the character of the Mass as an offering to God.[40]

For a confirmation of his thesis Jungmann refers to the debate about the eastward position in the Anglican Oxford Movement of the nineteenth century. The rubrics of the *Book of Common Prayer* of 1552 and 1661–1662 for Holy Communion state that 'the Priest standing *at the north side* of the *Table* shall say the Lords Prayer.'[41] The standard interpretation given already in the sixteenth century was that the minister should read the prayers standing at the left side of a table (in an oriented chancel). This practice was no doubt motivated by the intention to avoid any association with the Catholic Mass and its sacrificial character, a doctrine that was rejected in the authoritative 'Articles of Religion' of 1562 (1571); that is also the reason why traditional vestments were discarded.[42] When the High Churchman Charles Wheatly produced a new edition of his *Rational Illustration of the Book of Common Prayer* in 1720, he added a frontispiece depicting a priest standing in surplice and academic hood at the north end of a stone altar. In the clouds there is Jesus Christ standing at the north end of the heavenly altar, offering the same sacrifice. Being part of a Catholicising movement in the Church of England, Wheatly was familiar with Eastern Christian rites and attempted to restore the sacrificial understanding of the Eucharist, based on a reading of the Letter to the

[40] Jungmann, review of Nußbaum, 448.

[41] F. E. Brightman, *The English Rite: Being a Synopsis of the Sources and Revisions of the Book of Common Prayer with an Introduction and an Appendix*, 2d ed. (1921; reprint, Farnborough: Gregg International, 1970), 2:641.

[42] The thirty-nine articles are found conveniently in C. Hardwick, *A History of the Articles of Religion* (Cambridge: J. Deighton, 1851), 265–323, and G. Bray, ed., *Documents of the English Reformation* (Cambridge: James Clarke, 1994), 285–309; cf. the study of F. Clark, *Eucharistic Sacrifice and the Reformation*, 2d ed. (Oxford: Blackwell, 1967) on the eucharistic sacrifice and the Reformation.

Hebrews. At the same time, he wanted to remain faithful to the rubrics of the *Book of Common Prayer*. However, as Kenneth Stevenson remarks: 'Although Thomas Cranmer's eucharistic views are much disputed even today, they would not have coincided with those of Charles Wheatly, who so readily (and artistically) reinterprets the rite of the 1662 Prayer Book.'[43]

Alf Härdelin shows that for the Oxford Movement the eastward position was a crucial element in their efforts to restore the Catholic heritage to the Church of England, because it was taken to express the sacrificial character of the Eucharist and constitute liturgical worship as a 'God-ward act'. The common direction of liturgical prayer had a singular importance in the Tractarians' campaign against the rationalism of contemporary Anglican theology.[44] From their earliest years, the Tractarians worked with great vigour, both in writing and in practice, for the restoration of the eastward position. W. J. E. Bennett insisted that in order to evoke the doctrine of the eucharistic sacrifice, it was necessary for him to stand 'as a Priest—and before an Altar, as an Altar'. How significant the eastward position was for the Oxford Movement can be perceived from the posthumous *Remains* of Hurrell Froude. John Keble wrote in his preface to the second volume that Froude 'thought very seriously of the importance of those arrangements in Divine Service, which tend most to remind the worshipper that God's house is a house of prayer and spiritual sacrifice, not of mere instruction'.[45]

[43] K. Stevenson, *Eucharist and Offering* (New York: Pueblo, 1986), 3, cf. 159–60.

[44] Cf. A. Härdelin, *The Tractarian Understanding of the Eucharist*, AUU 8 (Uppsala: Almqvist and Wiksell, 1965), 309–12.

[45] The quotations from Bennett's *Farewell Letter* and Keble's preface to the second volume of Froude's *Remains* are found in ibid., 310.

John Henry Newman was hard pressed to keep to the normative application of the rubrics of the *Book of Common Prayer*, since any alteration of the established customs would have added fuel to the controversy about the Oxford Movement. It is reported that Newman always stood at the 'north end', that is, on the left side of the altar, when he celebrated Holy Communion.[46] In contrast, Isaac Williams, Newman's first curate in the parish church of Littlemore near Oxford, published a keen attack against the position of the minister at the 'north end' and made a case for facing east in the liturgy. For Williams, as for other Tractarians, this liturgical gesture was of such consequence, because they saw it intrinsically related to doctrine; in their eyes it stood for a basic theological perspective. The eastward position was considered, if not the only, certainly the key sign for understanding the eucharistic sacrifice as a 'God-ward act'. It was a central element in the Tractarians' fight against the rationalism then prevalent in Anglican theology. In the Anglo-Catholic movement, the common direction of prayer gained a significance that went far beyond the Ritualist controversies of the later nineteenth century with its famous trials concerning ceremonial in the Church of England. The Tractarians' emphasis on prayer facing east can only be understood in the context of their opposition to the rationalist theology of their age and the intense reaction of the ecclesiastical establishment.[47]

If we bear in mind the meaning that common direction of prayer had for the liturgical renewal of Anglicanism in the

---

[46] In 1841, Newman wrote to the Anglican Bishop of Oxford: 'I have left many things, which I did not like, and which most other persons would have altered': J. H. Newman, *The Via Media of the Anglican Church* (London: Basil Montagu Pickering, 1877), 2:405.

[47] This point is brought home by Härdelin, *Tractarian Understanding*, 300–315.

decades following the Oxford Movement, it is understandable that the introduction of the celebration *versus populum* into Anglican churches in the 1960s was met with profound reservations. For example, a contribution by John Macquarrie sheds light on the historical weight the eastward position has enjoyed in Anglicanism. Macquarrie sees in the 'excessive subjectivism' of our time a serious threat for theology and worship. This subjectivist attitude is conveyed by the newly adopted position of the celebrant facing the people at the Eucharist. Macquarrie takes issue with John A. T. Robinson, who, in his well-known book *Honest to God*, favours the celebration *versus populum* because it focuses 'attention upon a point in the middle'. For Macquarrie, this subjectivism is at the cost of the 'objective' dimension of the Eucharist, which is symbolised 'when priest and people together are directing themselves to God who is always ahead of us and always calling us to go out beyond ourselves into the venture of faith'. [48]

Jungmann does not spell out his idea of an intrinsic connection between the understanding of the Eucharist as a sacrifice and the common direction of priest and people. This would obviously require further in-depth study that cannot be done here. Nonetheless, Jungmann's thesis seems very plausible. Since the third century, the Eucharist has been named *prosphora*, *anaphora*, and *oblatio*, terms that articulate the idea of 'bringing to', 'presenting', and thus of a movement towards God. [49] As Gamber points out:

---

[48] Macquarrie, 'Subjectivity and Objectivity', 158.

[49] Cf. Jungmann, 'Der neue Altar', 377, and J. Betz, 'Die Prosphora in der patristischen Theologie', in *Opfer Christi und Opfer der Kirche: Die Lehre vom Meßopfer als Mysteriengedächtnis in der Theologie der Gegenwart*, ed. B. Neunheuser (Düsseldorf: Patmos, 1960), 99–116.

> The person who is doing the offering is facing the one who
> is receiving the offering; thus, he stands *before* the altar, po-
> sitioned *ad Dominum*, facing the Lord.[50]

Pastoral experience over the last four decades can teach us
that the understanding of the Mass as both the sacrifice of
Christ and the sacrifice of the Church has diminished considerably, if not faded away, among the faithful.[51] I do not
want to suggest that the sweeping triumph of the celebration *versus populum* is the only reason for this deplorable development. But the emphasis on the meal aspect of the
Eucharist that complemented the celebrant priest's turning
towards the people has been overdone and has failed to proclaim the Eucharist as 'a visible sacrifice (as the nature of
man demands)'.[52] Conceiving of the Eucharist as a meal *in
contrast* to a sacrifice is a fabricated dualism that, from the

---

[50] K. Gamber, *The Reform of the Roman Liturgy: Its Problems and Backgrounds*,
trans. K. D. Grimm (San Juan Capistrano, Calif.: Una Voce Press, 1993), 178.

[51] Cf. the analysis of R. J. Schreiter, *Constructing Local Theologies* (London:
SCM, 1985), 67: 'Codes provide the basic rules for the exercise of the sign
function. They are, so to speak, the "grammar" of culture texts. They encom-
pass the rules of action of a culture, of what is done and what is not to be
done. In so doing, they not only define the range of activity of the sign, but
can also tell us something of basic messages. Consider, for example, the change
in code for relations to the Eucharist sign. When the Eucharist began to be
celebrated by Roman Catholics with the priest facing the people, the sign
function of the Eucharist underwent change. The sacrificial element of the
Eucharist was weakened in favor of the meal aspect. The altar as sign was
shifted in the code from being the point where God and humanity met in
sacrificial communication to the table of the eucharistic meal.'

[52] Council of Trent (1562): DS 1740, quoted in the *Catechism of the Catholic
Church*, no. 1366. The sacrificial understanding of the Mass has been restated
clearly by Pope John Paul II, Encyclical Letter *Ecclesia de Eucharistia* (Vatican
City: Libreria Editrice Vaticana, 2003), 14–19, nos. 11–14. Cf. the observations of Jungmann, *Messe im Gottesvolk*, 23–24.

perspective of the liturgical tradition, is absurd.[53] 'The Mass is at the same time, and inseparably, the sacrificial memorial in which the sacrifice of the cross is perpetuated and the sacred banquet of communion with the Lord's body and blood',[54] as the *Catechism of the Catholic Church* states clearly, and these two aspects cannot be isolated from each other. The sacrificial character of the Eucharist must find an adequate expression in the actual rite. Not even the best mystagogical catechesis can make up for the decline in the understanding of the Mass among Catholics, if the liturgical celebration sends out signs to the contrary.

c. Adoration and contemplation

Finally, I should like to consider Max Thurian's reflections published in *Notitiae*, the organ of the Congregation for

[53] Cf. Bouyer's postscript to K. Gamber, *Tournés vers le Seigneur! (Zum Herrn hin!)*, trans. S. Wallon (Le Barroux: Sainte-Madeleine, 1993), 67: 'Il n'y a jamais eu, dans aucune religion, un sacrifice qui ne soit pas un repas, mais un repas *sacré*: reconnu comme enveloppant le mystère d'une spéciale présence et communication divine.'

[54] *Catechism of the Catholic Church*, no. 1382. Among recent contributions to the theology of the eucharistic sacrifice, see Betz, 'Die Prosphora in der patristischen Theologie'; Jungmann, *Messe im Gottesvolk*, 7–27; H. Moll, *Die Lehre von der Eucharistie als Opfer: Eine dogmengeschichtliche Untersuchung vom Neuen Testament bis Irenäus von Lyon*, Theoph 26 (Cologne: Hanstein, 1975); J. Betz, *Eucharistie: In der Schrift und Patristik*, HDG 4/4a (Freiburg: Herder, 1979); R. P. C. Hanson, *Eucharistic Offering in the Early Church*, GLS 19 (Bramcote: Grove Books, 1979); R. Williams, *Eucharistic Sacrifice: The Roots of a Metaphor*, GLS 31 (Bramcote: Grove Books, 1982); B. D. Spinks, 'Eucharistic Offering in the East Syrian Anaphoras', *OCP* 50 (1984): 347–71; and Stevenson, *Eucharist and Offering* (1986), as well as the collected papers in A. Gerhards and K. Richter, eds., *Das Opfer: Biblischer Anspruch und liturgische Gestalt*, QD 186 (Freiburg: Herder, 2000). Ratzinger, 'Theologie der Liturgie', *FKTh* 18 (2002): 1–13, points to the desiderata of the contemporary discussion and stresses that much theological reflection is still to be done.

Divine Worship. Thurian is very candid about the deficiencies of contemporary liturgical life: apathy towards worship,
boredom, lack of vitality, and participation. The basic problem is the fact that the celebration of the liturgy is often
devoid of its character as mystery. Thurian points to the symbols and images used in the liturgical tradition of the Church
to convey a sense of the Eucharist as an act of thanksgiving,
a consecration, a memorial, and an offering accompanied by
intercessions. The eucharistic liturgy invites the celebrant
priests and the faithful to turn towards the altar of the Lord
in an attitude of adoration and contemplation. This must be
made visible in the shape of the liturgical celebration:

> Regardless of the church's architectural structure, these two
> complementary attitudes of the liturgy must always be re-
> spected: the face-to-face dialogue of the Liturgy of the Word
> and the contemplative orientation of the Liturgy of the Eu-
> charist. The whole celebration is often conducted as if it
> were a conversation and dialogue in which there is no lon-
> ger any room for adoration, contemplation and silence. The
> fact that the celebrants and faithful constantly face each other
> closes the liturgy in on itself. On the other hand, a sound
> celebration, which takes into account the pre-eminence of
> the altar, the discretion of the celebrants' ministry, the ori-
> entation of everyone towards the Lord and the adoration of
> his presence signified in the symbols and realised by the sac-
> rament, confers on the liturgy that contemplative atmo-
> sphere without which it risks being a tiresome religious
> disquisition, a useless community distraction, a sort of rig-
> marole [un fatigant bavardage religieux, une vaine agitation
> communautaire, *una specie di filastrocca*].[55]

[55] Translating M. Thurian, 'La Liturgie, contemplation du mystère', *Not* 32
(1996): 692. For the translation I am indebted to the weekly English-language
edition of *L'Osservatore Romano*, 24 July 1996, 2.

Thurian favours the classical Western basilica plan with a large rectangular nave ending in a semicircular apse. He regards this layout of the liturgical space as most fitting for a community on its pilgrimage towards the Lord, since it conveys the dynamism of a people's expectation and encounter with its Lord. Architectural arrangements certainly vary according to the place and circumstances; but they should always embody the movement towards the place of the Lord's offering and presence, that is, the altar and the tabernacle:

> Wherever tradition has left stupendous altars placed against the apse, this arrangement could be respected by dividing the celebration into a face-to-face between the celebrants and the community for the Liturgy of the Word and a common orientation towards the altar from the time of the offertory to the Amen of the Eucharistic Prayer.[56]

In this context Thurian criticises the widespread practice of putting the chairs for the celebrant and his assistants immediately behind the altar. Thus priests and people will face each other throughout the liturgical celebration:

> [This arrangement] turns the assembly in on itself and prevents the contemplative orientation of the whole community in adoration towards the symbolic place of the Lord's presence and in eschatological expectation of his return. The urgent need for the Church's liturgy today is to arrange everything so as to foster in the greatest possible way the contemplative adoration of the Lord, who reveals himself to his people in Word and Sacrament, and whose humble, unobtrusive servants are the celebrants.[57]

---

[56] Translating Thurian, 'La Liturgie', 693.
[57] Translating ibid., 694.

Thurian adds that this contemplative and eschatological orientation can be clearly perceived in the Pope's private chapel, where he celebrates Mass every morning, the whole congregation being turned with him towards the altar[58] and adoring the Real Presence of Christ.

[58] 'On peut ressentir très fortement cette orientation contemplative et eschatologique dans la chapelle privée du Pape, où il célèbre la messe chaque matin, d'abord à son siège un peu en avant du premier rang des participants, tournés avec lui vers l'autel, puis à l'autel même en tête de la petite assemblée qui adore avec lui le Christ réellement présent': ibid., 694.

IV

Turning to the Lord

The history of the *celebratio versus populum* in the proper sense began in the late Middle Ages and the Renaissance, when the Christian principle of praying towards the east was little understood and began to fade away. De Blaauw records the significant stages in this development and shows how misconceptions about early Roman church architecture could arise when the principle of orientation was no longer understood.[1] Nonetheless, the common direction of liturgical prayer was retained, with very few exceptions.[2] The idea that the priest should face the people during the celebration of Mass only gained currency in the Catholic Enlightenment of the eighteenth century. The rationalist *Zeitgeist* also affected liturgical practice and thought. Christian worship was supposed to be useful for the moral edification of the individual and for the building of society. Needless to say, this was at the expense of its latreutic and mystical nature; hence the espousal of the aesthetic ideal of 'noble simplicity'

---

[1] Cf. S. de Blaauw, *Met het oog op het licht: Een vergeten principe in de oriëntatie van het vroegchristelijk kerkgebouw*, Nijmeegse Kunsthistorische Cahiers 2 (Nijmegen: Nijmegen University Press, 2000), 43–51.

[2] It is reported that Spanish missionaries from the mendicant orders as an experiment celebrated the Mass *versus populum* for the Aztec converts of central Mexico; cf. J. Lara, 'Versus Populum Revisited', *Worship* 68 (1994): 219–20.

and the demand for the rites to be simplified and intelligible. These tendencies coincided with various currents in Catholicism that endorsed similar ideas, though partly for different motives, such as Jansenism and Josephism. However, it would seem that the call for Mass facing the people was hardly put into practice.[3]

As Bouyer relates from his own experience, the pioneers of the Liturgical Movement in the twentieth century had two chief motives for promoting the celebration of Mass *versus populum*. First, they wished the readings to be delivered facing the people. Their problem was that, according to the rubrics for low Mass, the priest had to read the Epistle and Gospel from the Missal on the altar. Since they wanted to proclaim the Word of God towards the people and, at the same time, follow the rubrics, the only option was to celebrate the whole Mass *versus populum*, as was provided for by the Missal of Pope Saint Pius V to cover the particular arrangement of the major Roman basilicas. The instruction *Inter Oecumenici* of 1964 allowed the reading of the Epistle and Gospel from a pulpit or ambo. With this instruction the first incentive for Mass facing the people became no longer valid. There was, however, another reason motivating the

---

[3] Still useful is W. Trapp, *Vorgeschichte und Ursprung der liturgischen Bewegung vorwiegend in Hinsicht auf das deutsche Sprachgebiet* (1940; reprinted, Münster: Antiquariat Stenderhoff, 1979); cf. also O. Nußbaum, *Der Standort des Liturgen am christlichen Altar vor dem Jahre 1000: Eine archäologische und liturgiegeschichtliche Untersuchung*, Theoph 18 (Bonn: Hanstein, 1965), 1:18–23; and A. Nichols, *Looking at the Liturgy: A Critical View of Its Contemporary Form* (San Francisco: Ignatius Press, 1996), 17–23. A radical advocate of this 'Enlightenment liturgy' was Vitus Anton Winter; see J. Steiner, *Liturgiereform in der Aufklärungszeit: Eine Darstellung am Beispiel Vitus Anton Winters*, FThSt 100 (Freiburg: Herder, 1976). On Josephist ideas about liturgy, see H. Hollerweger, *Die Reform des Gottesdienstes zur Zeit des Josephinismus in Österreich*, StPaLi 1 (Regensburg: Pustet, 1976).

Liturgical Movement, namely, the intention to reclaim the perception of the Eucharist as a sacred banquet, which it was thought had been lost sight of. The celebration of Mass facing the people was seen as an adequate way of repairing this loss. As has been noted in the course of my argument, the eucharistic liturgy is not a community meal in the strict sense. Moreover, there could be nothing more alien to a real meal than the positioning of the celebrant *versus populum*, with the altar as an undesirable barrier between clergy and laity. Be that as it may, today our situation is very different from that of the first half of the twentieth century, since the meal aspect of the Eucharist has become common property, and it is its sacrificial character that needs to be recovered.[4]

Jungmann remarked already in 1967 that 'now the pendulum must also be allowed to swing to the other end.'[5] He emphasises that Christ is truly in our midst but that we are directed with him to the Father. The common orientation in prayer has indisputable benefits, because it is a real symbol of this movement towards God, which is inherent in the traditional terms for the Eucharist, such as *prosphora* and *oblatio*. We present our prayers and offerings through Christ to the Father. This procession is led by the priest, who along with the faithful turns towards the transcendent God who is to come. Recalling Cardinal Lercaro's letter of 25 January 1966, which demanded prudence and caution, Jungmann ends with

[4] Cf. L. Bouyer, *Liturgy and Architecture* (Notre Dame, Ind.: University of Notre Dame Press, 1967), 106–11, followed by C. Napier, 'The Altar in the Contemporary Church', *CleR* 57 (1972): 630. On the history of the *celebratio versus populum* in the Liturgical Movement of the twentieth century, see B. Neunheuser, 'Eucharistiefeier am Altare *versus populum*: Geschichte und Problematik', in *Florentissima proles Ecclesiae: Miscellanea hagiographica, historica et liturgica Reginaldo Grégoire O.S.B. XII lustra complenti oblata*, ed. D. Gobbi (Trento: Civis, 1996), 433–43.

[5] Translating J. A. Jungmann, 'Der neue Altar', *Der Seelsorger* 37 (1967): 379.

the warning that 'one should not cast to the wind the lesson of history.'[6]

By way of concluding this study, I shall consider a proposal on the celebration of Mass today that has been put forward by various authors. There is a widespread consensus that the dialogue parts between priest and people and the proclamation of the Word of God require a face-to-face position. So the Introductory Rites and the Liturgy of the Word should best be conducted from the sedilia and the ambo, as is now the case. It should also be taken for granted that for parts of the Communion Rite and for the Concluding Rite the priest faces the people, according to the rubrics of the renewed *Missale Romanum*. However, for the Liturgy of the Eucharist in the strict sense, in particular the canon, it is more than fitting that the whole congregation, including the celebrant, be directed towards the Lord, and that is expressed by turning towards the altar—whether it is actually oriented or only indicates the 'liturgical' east. Hence the celebrant should not face the people during this part of the Mass.[7]

---

[6] Translating ibid., 380; cf. J. A. Jungmann, review of O. Nußbaum, *Der Standort des Liturgen am christlichen Altar vor dem Jahre 1000*, ZKTh 88 (1966): 449.

[7] Bouyer, *Liturgy and Architecture*, 103–4, notes that this should also obtain for the bidding prayers, which are directed to God, in the same way as the Eucharistic Prayer. A distinction between the position of the celebrant at the altar during the Liturgy of the Word and during the Liturgy of the Eucharist is also championed by M. Metzger, 'La Place des liturges à l'autel', *RevSR* 45 (1971): 143; Napier, 'Altar in the Contemporary Church', 630; K. Gamber, *Tournés vers le Seigneur! (Zum Herrn hin!)*, trans. S. Wallon (Le Barroux: Sainte-Madeleine, 1993), 51–52; and M. Thurian, 'La Liturgie, contemplation du mystère', *Not* 32 (1996): 692–93. M. Kunzler, 'La liturgia all'inizio del Terzo Millennio', in *Il Concilio Vaticano II: Recezione e attualità alla luce del Giubileo*, ed. R. Fisichella (Milan: San Paolo, 2000), 228–29, also affirms the merits of the celebration *ad Dominum*.

This is not the place to enter into a detailed discussion of how this proposal could or should be put into practice. At any rate, it is not beside the point to recommend that the priest should pray facing the altar in those (usually historic) churches where the altar is the dominating artistic feature of the chapel or even of the whole building. The splendid altars in the churches of the West from the late Middle Ages to the Baroque are part of a development that clearly goes beyond the altar arrangements of the first millennium, still found today in churches of the Byzantine and the Oriental traditions. Such magnificent altars serve the purpose of the liturgy very well, that is to say, the praise and glory of God and the sacramental representation of his saving work for the faithful who are assembled for prayer and offering. As Cardinal Ratzinger reminds us: '[T]he altar is the place where heaven is opened up. It does not close off the church, but opens it up—and leads it into the eternal liturgy.' [8]

This suggested combination of priest and people facing each other during the Liturgy of the Word and turning jointly towards the altar during the Liturgy of the Eucharist is not only a legitimate option in the *Novus Ordo Missae* of Pope Paul VI; it has also been approved explicitly by the Roman Congregation for Divine Worship. The *Notitiae* editorial already referred to lists five guiding points on the position of the celebrant, of which two are relevant to our argument. One point applies in particular to historic churches that were often lavished with fine artistic decorations in order to impress on the worshippers the greatness and splendour of God's work of salvation. The editorial states:

---

[8] J. Ratzinger, *The Spirit of the Liturgy*, trans. J. Saward (San Francisco: Ignatius Press, 2000), 71.

The arrangement of the altar *versus populum* is certainly a
desideratum of the current liturgical legislation. It is not,
however, an absolute value to be held above all others. Cases
must be considered in which the sanctuary does not allow
for the placing of an altar facing the people or in which it
would not be possible to maintain the existing altar with its
ornamentation intact and at the same time install a forward-
facing altar that could be seen as the principal altar. In such
cases it is more faithful to the nature of the liturgy to celebrate at the existing altar, back to the people, than to maintain two altars in the same sanctuary. The principle of there
being only one altar [unicità dell' altare] is theologically more
important than the practice of celebrating facing the people.[9]

Alfred Lorenzer emphasises that the altar of a church is the
focal point of the building's 'sense-structure' (*Sinngefüge*) as
well as of its spatial structure. If the position of the altar is
changed, both the spatial structure and the sense-structure
of the church are damaged, if not destroyed. Putting up free-
standing 'people's altars' in historic churches made superflu-
ous a significant part of the building, which until then was
full of sacred meaning and artistic value. What used to be
essential for the sacred symbolism of the church has been
reduced to a 'sense-ruin' (*Sinnruine*). This radical change is
yet more dramatic than the decline of traditional Latin sacred music, for in this case no visible sign remains of the loss,
whereas the architectural onslaught made in the name of liturgical reform leaves behind a destroyed space, a continu-
ally present 'sense-ruin'.[10] The desire to preserve ancient

[9] Translating Congregatio de Cultu Divino et Disciplina Sacramentorum,
'Editoriale: Pregare "ad orientem versus"', *Not* 29 (1993): 249.
[10] Cf. A. Lorenzer, *Das Konzil der Buchhalter: Die Zerstörung der Sinnlichkeit:
Eine Religionskritik*, unabridged ed. (Frankfurt am Main: Fischer-Taschenbuch-
Verlag, 1984), 200–202: 'Der Altar ist als Schwerpunkt des "Sinngefüges Kirche"

churches is not only a matter of cultural heritage but is demanded also by the reform of the liturgy properly understood. One cannot appeal to the Second Vatican Council for a justification of the radical alterations that historic churches have undergone in recent times.[11] It is entirely consistent with the intention of Vatican II that the Congregation for Divine Worship gives preference to the celebration at an existing (high) altar over the construction of another altar directed towards the people.

---

notwendig "räumlicher Schwerpunkt", das heißt, sein Platz und seine Gestalt sind konstitutiv für die Raumstruktur. Verlagert man seinen Ort, so beeinträchtigt und zerstört man die Raumstruktur, bringt den Raum als Sinngestalt "zum Einsturz".... Was bedeutet es, daß das liturgische Geschehen verkürzt wird um eine bislang in Dienst genommene Kunst, um eine Symbolebene, nämlich den sakral bedeutungsvollen Raum? ... Ein desymbolisierter Raum bleibt gegenwärtig als "Sinnruine".' A. Lorenzer, '"Sacrosanctum Concilium": Der Anfang der "Buchhalterei": Betrachtungen aus psychoanalytisch-kulturkritischer Sicht', in *Gottesdienst–Kirche–Gesellschaft: Interdisziplinäre und ökumenische Standortbestimmungen nach 25 Jahren Liturgiereform*, ed. H. Becker, B.J. Hilberath, and U. Willers, PiLi 5 (St. Ottilien: EOS-Verlag, 1991), 159, cautions: 'Man steigt nicht ungestraft aus dem geschichtlichen Zusammenhang aus, indem man das Bestehende einfach verleugnet.' A similar word of warning can already be found in J. Ratzinger, 'Catholicism after the Council', trans. P. Russell, *The Furrow* 18 (1967): 13: 'There is a law of continuity which we transgress at our peril.' Cf. the observations on the present situation by A. Gerhards, '"Der Kirchenraum als Liturge": Anregungen zu einem anderen Dialog von Kunst und Kirche', in *Heiliger Raum: Architektur, Kunst und Liturgie in mittelalterlichen Kathedralen und Stiftskirchen*, ed. F. Kohlschein and P. Wünsche, LWQF 82 (Münster: Aschendorff, 1998), 230–33.

[11] Cf. the well-documented argument of A. Odenthal, 'Denkmalpflege als Postulat der Liturgiereform', *LJ* 42 (1992): 249–59, who objects to Lorenzer on this point. On the sweeping reordering of churches and its consequences for the protection of national and cultural heritage, see N. Gauss, 'Kirchenerweiterungen in Österreich: Versuch einer Typologie: Eine Zwischenbilanz 25 Jahre nach dem Zweiten Vatikanum', *ÖZKD* 44 (1990): 1–25, and G. Klötzl, '"Zwingende liturgische Notwendigkeit" zu Altarraumumbauten? Bemerkungen zu § 5 Absatz 4 Denkmalschutzgesetz' *ÖZKD* 46 (1992): 38–43.

In addition, the Congregation also recognises the theological foundation for the common direction of liturgical prayer. What is at issue is the character of the Eucharist as prayer and offering addressed to God:

> It is fitting to explain clearly that the expression 'to celebrate facing the people' has no theological sense but is only a topographical concept. Every celebration of the Eucharist is 'ad laudem et gloriam nominis Dei, ad utilitatem quoque nostram, totiusque Ecclesiae suae sanctae'. Theologically, therefore, the Mass is always facing God and facing the people. In the form of celebration one must be careful to avoid confounding theology and topography, especially when the priest is at the altar. It is only in the dialogues from the altar that the priest speaks to the people. All the rest is prayer to the Father, through the mediation of Christ in the Holy Spirit. This theology must be visible.[12]

Reclaiming the common direction of prayer seems most desirable for the liturgical life and, hence, for the welfare of the Church. The historical and theological arguments presented in this study will, I hope, serve to revive this ancient tradition. In this liturgical gesture the Church turns to her source of life, the risen and ascended Lord, whose return she desires and expects.

[12] Translating Congregatio de Cultu Divino et Disciplina Sacramentorum, 'Editoriale', 249.

ABBREVIATIONS

AAS	*Acta Apostolicae Sedis*
ALW	*Archiv für Liturgiewissenschaft*
APAW.PH	Abhandlungen der Königlich-Preußischen Akademie der Wissenschaften. Philosophisch-historische Klasse
AugL	*Augustinus-Lexikon*
AUU	Acta Universitatis Upsalensis
BEFAR	Bibliothèque des écoles françaises d'Athènes et de Rome
BJSt	Brown Judaic Studies
CCCIC	*Communicationes*
CChr.CM	Corpus Christianorum. Continuatio Mediaevalis
CChr.SL	Corpus Christianorum. Series Latina
CleR	*Clergy Review*
CSCO	Corpus Scriptorum Christianorum Orientalium
CSEL	Corpus Scriptorum Ecclesiasticorum Latinorum
CStS	Collected Studies Series
DS	*Enchiridion symbolorum*, edited by H. Denzinger and A. Schönmetzer
FKGCA	Forschungen zur Kunstgeschichte und christlichen Archäologie
FKTh	*Forum Katholische Theologie*
FThSt	Freiburger theologische Studien
GCS	Die griechischen christlichen Schriftsteller der ersten drei Jahrhunderte
GdK	Gottesdienst der Kirche

Turning towards the Lord

GLS	Grove Liturgical Study
GrTS	Grazer theologische Studien
HBS	Henry Bradshaw Society
HDG	Handbuch der Dogmengeschichte
HerKor	*Herder-Korrespondenz*
HlD	*Heiliger Dienst*
HUCA	*Hebrew Union College Annual*
IkaZ	*Internationale katholische Zeitschrift Communio*
IThS	Innsbrucker Theologische Studien
JAC	*Jahrbuch für Antike und Christentum*
JAC.E	Jahrbuch für Antike und Christentum. Ergänzungsband
JLH	*Jahrbuch für Liturgik und Hymnologie*
JSOT	*Journal for the Study of the Old Testament*
JThS	*Journal of Theological Studies*
KKTS	Konfessionskundliche und kontroverstheologische Studien
LF	Liturgiegeschichtliche Forschungen
LJ	*Liturgisches Jahrbuch*
LWQF	Liturgiewissenschaftliche Quellen und Forschungen
MGH.Cap	Monumenta Germaniae Historica. Capitularia Regum Francorum
MGH.SRM	Monumenta Germaniae Historica. Scriptores rerum Merovingicarum
MThS.H	Münchener theologische Studien. Historische Abteilung
NBl	*New Blackfriars*
Not	*Notitiae*
OCA	Orientalia Christiana Analecta
OCP	*Orientalia Christiana Periodica*
OR	*Les Ordines Romani du haut moyen âge*, edited by M. Andrieu (Louvain: Peeters, 1948–1961)

OrSyr	*L'Orient Syrien*
ÖZKD	*Österreichische Zeitschrift für Kunst und Denkmalpflege*
PEQ	*Palestine Exploration Quarterly*
PG	Patrologiae Cursus Completus, accurante J.-P. Migne. Series Graeca
PiLi	Pietas liturgica
PL	Patrologiae Cursus Completus, accurante J.-P. Migne. Series Latina
QD	Quaestiones Disputatae
RAC	*Reallexikon für Antike und Christentum*
RevSR	*Revue des sciences religieuses*
RivAC	*Rivista di Archeologia Cristiana*
RJ	Römisches Jahrbuch der Bibliotheca Hertziana
SC	Sources Chrétiennes
SEAug	Studia ephemerides 'Augustinianum'
SFNF	Studia Friburgensia. Neue Folge
SPLi	Studia patristica et liturgica
StMed	*Studi medievali*
StPaLi	Studien zur Pastoralliturgie
StPatr	*Studia Patristica*
Theoph	Theophaneia
ThPh	*Theologie und Philosophie*
ThRv	*Theologische Revue*
UTB	Uni-Taschenbücher
UVK	*Una-Voce-Korrespondenz*
VigChr	*Vigiliae Christianae*
WoodSt	Woodbrooke Studies
WUNT	Wissenschaftliche Untersuchungen zum Neuen Testament
ZDPV	*Zeitschrift des Deutschen Palästina-Vereins*
ZKG	*Zeitschrift für Kirchengeschichte*
ZKTh	*Zeitschrift für Katholische Theologie*

ILLUSTRATIONS

Figure 1: The Last Supper as depicted on a mosaic in S. Apollinare Nuovo, Ravenna (around 520), Buch-Kunstverlag Ettal. Best.-Nr. 4524.

Figure 2: Ground plan (simplified) of the Christian building in Dura-Europos. Kraeling, C. H. *The Christian Building.* The Excavations at Dura-Europos. Final Report 8, pt. 2. New Haven: Dura-Europos Publications, 1967. Page 4.

Figure 3: Early Syrian churches with a *bema*. Left the church of Qirqbīze (fourth century) with a single nave, right the basilica of Sinhār (mid-fourth century). Tchalenko, G. *Villages antiques de la Syrie du Nord: Le Massif du Bélus à l'époque romaine.* 3 vols. Paris: P. Geuthner, 1953–1958. Volume 2, Plate IX.

Figure 4: Ground plan of St. Peter's during the pontificate of Symmachus (498–514), according to S. de Blaauw, who locates the main altar within the precinct of the tomb. Blaauw, S. de. *Cultus et decor. Liturgia e architettura nella Roma tardoantica e medievale. Basilica Salvatoris, Sanctae Mariae, Sancti Petri.* 2 vols. Vatican City: Biblioteca Apostolica Vaticana, 1994. Volume 2, Figure 19.

Figure 5: Longitudinal section (schematic) of the sanctuary of St. Peter's in the seventh century. The dotted line indicates the floor-level of the Constantinian apse. Blaauw, S. de. *Cultus et decor. Liturgia e architettura nella Roma tardoantica e medievale. Basilica Salvatoris, Sanctae Mariae, Sancti Petri.* 2

vols. Vatican City: Biblioteca Apostolica Vaticana, 1994. Volume 2, Figure 24.

Figure 6: The mosaic of Thabarca and an axiometric reconstruction of the church according to J. B. Ward-Perkins and R. G. Goodchild. Duval, N. 'Commentaire topographique et archéologique'. In *Augustin Prédicateur (395–411): Actes du Colloque International de Chantilly (5–7 septembre 1996)*, edited by G. Madec, 171–214. Collection des Études Augustiniennes, Série Antiquité 159. Paris: Institut d'Études Augustiniennes, 1998. Page 207.

BIBLIOGRAPHY

I have not included in this bibliography ancient sources (which are quoted according to their current critical editions) and their translations (which are taken from the *Library of Ante-Nicene, Nicene and Post-Nicene Fathers* and the *Ancient Christian Writers* series).

Arbeiter, A. *Alt-St. Peter in Geschichte und Wissenschaft: Abfolge der Bauten, Rekonstruktion, Architekturprogramm*. Berlin: Mann, 1988.

Badger, G. P. *The Nestorians and Their Rituals*. 2 vols. 1852. Reprint, London: Darf, 1987.

Balthasar, H. U. von. 'Die Würde der Liturgie'. *IkaZ* 7 (1978): 481–87.

Bauer, W. *Orthodoxy and Heresy in Earliest Christianity*. Translated by a team from the Philadelphia Seminar on Christian Origins. Edited by R. A. Kraft and G. Krodel. Philadelphia: Fortress Press, 1971.

Belting-Ihm, C. *Die Programme der christlichen Apsismalerei vom 4. Jahrhundert bis zur Mitte des 8. Jahrhunderts*. FKGCA 4. 2d ed. Stuttgart: Steiner, 1992.

Berger, P. L. *A Far Glory: The Quest for Faith in an Age of Credulity*. New York: Free Press, 1992.

Betz, J. *Eucharistie: In der Schrift und Patristik*. HDG 4/4a. Freiburg: Herder, 1979.

_____. 'Die Prosphora in der patristischen Theologie'. In *Opfer Christi und Opfer der Kirche: Die Lehre vom Meßopfer als Mysteriengedächtnis in der Theologie der Gegenwart*, edited by B. Neunheuser, 99–116. Düsseldorf: Patmos, 1960.

Blaauw, S. de. 'Architecture and Liturgy in Late Antiquity and the Middle Ages'. *ALW* 33 (1991): 1–34.

———. *Cultus et decor: Liturgia e architettura nella Roma tardoantica e medievale: Basilica Salvatoris, Sanctae Mariae, Sancti Petri.* 2 vols. Vatican City: Biblioteca Apostolica Vaticana, 1994.

———. *Met het oog op het licht: Een vergeten principe in de oriëntatie van het vroegchristelijk kerkgebouw.* Nijmeegse Kunsthistorische Cahiers 2. Nijmegen: Nijmegen University Press, 2000.

Borromeo, C. *Instructiones fabricae et supellectilis ecclesiasticae, Cap. X, De cappella maiori.* Edited by S. della Torre and M. Marinelli. Translated by M. Marinelli. Monumenta studia instrumenta liturgica 8. Vatican City: Libreria Editrice Vaticana, 2000.

Bouyer, L. *Liturgy and Architecture.* Notre Dame, Ind.: University of Notre Dame Press, 1967.

———. *Rite and Man: The Sense of the Sacral and Christian Liturgy.* Translated by M. J. Costelloe. London: Burns and Oates, 1963.

Brandenburg, H. 'Altar und Grab: Zu einem Problem des Märtyrerkultes im 4. und 5. Jh'. In *Martyrium in Multidisciplinary Perspective: Memorial Louis Reekmans,* edited by M. Lamberigts and P. van Deun, 71–98. Louvain: Peeters, 1995.

Braun, J. *Der christliche Altar in seiner geschichtlichen Entwicklung.* 2 vols. Munich: Alte Meister Guenther Koch, 1924.

Bray, G., ed. *Documents of the English Reformation.* Cambridge: James Clarke, 1994.

Brightman, F. E. *The English Rite: Being a Synopsis of the Sources and Revisions of the Book of Common Prayer with an Introduction and an Appendix.* 2d ed. 2 vols. 1921. Reprint, Farnborough: Gregg International, 1970.

Bunge, G. *Earthen Vessels: The Practice of Personal Prayer according to the Patristic Tradition*. Translated by M. J. Miller. San Francisco: Ignatius Press, 2002.

Burkert, W. *Klassisches Altertum und antikes Christentum: Probleme einer übergreifenden Religionswissenschaft*. Hans-Lietzmann-Vorlesungen 1. Berlin: Walter de Gruyter, 1996.

Burkitt, F. C. Review of F. J. Dölger, *Sol salutis: Gebet und Gesang im christlichen Altertum*. Münster: Aschendorff, 1920. *JThS* 22 (1921): 283–86.

Cantoni, P. 'Per un "nuovo" movimento liturgico'. *Cristianità* 30 (2002): 5–18.

Catechism of the Catholic Church. London: Geoffrey Chapman, 1994.

Chadwick, H. 'New Sermons of St Augustine'. *JThS* NS 47 (1996): 69–91.

Clark, F. *Eucharistic Sacrifice and the Reformation*. 2d ed. Oxford: Blackwell, 1967.

Congregatio de Cultu Divino et Disciplina Sacramentorum. 'Editoriale: Pregare "ad orientem versus"'. *Not* 29 (1993): 245–49.

_____. 'Responsa ad quaestiones de nova *Institutione Generali Missalis Romani*'. *CCCIC* 32 (2000): 171–74.

Congregatio pro Ecclesiis Orientalibus. *Instruzione per l'applicazione delle prescrizioni liturgiche del Codice dei Canoni delle Chiese Orientali 'Il Padre incomprensibile'*. Vatican City: Libreria Editrice Vaticana, 1996.

Cullen, C. M., and J. W. Koterski. 'The New IGMR and Mass *versus Populum*'. *Homiletic and Pastoral Review*, June 2001, 51–54.

Cuming, G. J. *The Liturgy of St Mark, Edited from the Manuscripts with a Commentary*. OCA 234. Rome: Pontificium Institutum Studiorum Orientalium, 1990.

Documents on the Liturgy, 1963–1979: Conciliar, Papal, and Curial Texts. Collegeville, Minn.: Liturgical Press, 1982.

Dölger, F. J. *Sol salutis: Gebet und Gesang im christlichen Altertum: Mit besonderer Rücksicht auf die Ostung in Gebet und Liturgie.* 2d ed. LF 4/5. Münster: Aschendorff, 1925.

————. *Die Sonne der Gerechtigkeit und der Schwarze: Eine religionsgeschichtliche Studie zum Taufgelöbnis.* LF 2. Münster: Aschendorff, 1918.

Dolbeau, F. *Augustin d'Hippone: Vingt-Six Sermons au Peuple d'Afrique retrouvés à Mayence.* Collection des Études Augustiniennes, Série Antiquité 147. Paris: Institut d'Études Augustiniennes, 1996.

————. 'L'Oraison "Conuersi ad dominum . . .": Un Bilan provisoire des recensions existantes'. *ALW* 41 (1999): 295–322.

Duval, N. 'L'Architecture chrétienne et les pratiques liturgiques en Jordanie en rapport avec la Palestine: Recherches nouvelles'. In *'Churches Built in Ancient Times': Recent Studies in Early Christian Architecture*, edited by K. Painter, 149–212. London: Society of Antiquaries, 1994.

————. 'Commentaire topographique et archéologique'. In *Augustin Prédicateur (395–411): Actes du Colloque International de Chantilly (5–7 septembre 1996)*, edited by G. Madec, 171–214. Collection des Études Augustiniennes, Série Antiquité 159. Paris: Institut d'Études Augustiniennes, 1998.

Fischer, B. 'Die Grundaussagen der Liturgie-Konstitution und ihre Rezeption in fünfundzwanzig Jahren'. In *Gottesdienst–Kirche–Gesellschaft: Interdisziplinäre und ökumenische Standortbestimmungen nach 25 Jahren Liturgiereform*, edited by H. Becker, B. J. Hilberath, and U. Willers, 417–28. PiLi 5. St. Ottilien: EOS-Verlag, 1991.

Frank, K.S. 'Maleachi 1, 10ff. in der frühen Väterdeutung: Ein Beitrag zu Opferterminologie und Opferverständnis in der alten Kirche'. *ThPh* 53 (1978): 70–78.

Gamber, K. *Liturgie und Kirchenbau: Studien zur Geschichte der Meßfeier und des Gotteshauses in der Frühzeit.* SPLi 6. Regensburg: Pustet, 1976.

_____. *The Modern Rite: Collected Essays on the Reform of the Liturgy.* Translated by H. Taylor. Farnborough: Saint Michael's Abbey Press, 2002.

_____. *The Reform of the Roman Liturgy: Its Problems and Backgrounds.* Translated by K.D. Grimm. San Juan Capistrano, Calif.: Una Voce Press, 1993.

_____. *Tournés vers le Seigneur! (Zum Herrn hin!).* Translated by S. Wallon. Le Barroux: Sainte-Madeleine, 1993.

Garriga, T. 'La sacra liturgia fonte e culmina della vita ecclesiale'. In *Il Concilio Vaticano II: Recezione e attualità alla luce del Giubileo,* edited by R. Fisichella, 46–65. Milan: San Paolo, 2000.

Gauss, N. 'Kirchenerweiterungen in Österreich: Versuch einer Typologie: Eine Zwischenbilanz 25 Jahre nach dem Zweiten Vatikanum'. *ÖZKD* 44 (1990): 1–25.

Gawlikowski, M. 'Eine neuentdeckte frühchristliche Kirche in Palmyra'. In *Syrien: Von den Aposteln zu den Kalifen,* edited by E.M. Ruprechtsberger, 150–57. Mainz: Von Zabern, 1993.

Gerhards, A. '"Blickt nach Osten!" Die Ausrichtung von Priester und Gemeinde bei der Eucharistie—eine kritische Reflexion nachkonziliarer Liturgiereform vor dem Hintergrund der Geschichte des Kirchenbaus'. In *Liturgia et Unitas: Liturgiewissenschaftliche und ökumenische Studien zur Eucharistie und zum gottesdienstlichen Leben in der Schweiz: Études liturgiques et oecuméniques sur l'Eucharistie et la vie liturgique en Suisse: In honorem Bruno Bürki,* edited by M.

Klöckener and A. Join-Lambert, 197–217. Fribourg: Univ.-Verl., and Geneva: Labor et Fides, 2001.

———. '"Der Kirchenraum als Liturge": Anregungen zu einem anderen Dialog von Kunst und Kirche'. In *Heiliger Raum: Architektur, Kunst und Liturgie in mittelalterlichen Kathedralen und Stiftskirchen*, edited by F. Kohlschein and P. Wünsche, 225–42. LWQF 82. Münster: Aschendorff, 1998.

———. 'Versus orientem—versus populum. Zum gegenwärtigen Diskussionsstand einer alten Streitfrage'. *ThRv* 98 (2002): 15–22.

Gerhards, A., and K. Richter, eds. *Das Opfer: Biblischer Anspruch und liturgische Gestalt.* QD 186. Freiburg: Herder, 2000.

Guidobaldi, F. 'L'inserimento delle chiese titolari di Roma nel tessuto urbano preesistente: Osservazioni ed implicazioni'. In *Quaeritur inventus colitur: Miscellanea in onore di Padre U. M. Fasola*, 382–96. Vatican City: Pontificio Istituto di archeologia cristiana, 1989.

Gy, P. M. '*L'Esprit de la liturgie* du Cardinal Ratzinger est-il fidèle au Concile, ou en réaction contre?' *La Maison-Dieu* 229 (2002): 171–78.

Härdelin, A. *The Tractarian Understanding of the Eucharist.* AUU 8. Uppsala: Almqvist and Wiksell, 1965.

Häußling, A. A. Review of U. M. Lang, 'Conversi ad Dominum: Zu Gebetsostung, Stellung des Liturgen am Altar und Kirchenbau', *FKTh* 16 (2000): 81–123. *ALW* 42 (2000): 156–57.

Hanson, R. P. C. *Eucharistic Offering in the Early Church.* GLS 19. Bramcote: Grove Books, 1979.

Harbert, B. 'Paradise and the Liturgy'. *NBl* 83 (2002): 30–41.

Hardwick, C. *A History of the Articles of Religion.* Cambridge: J. Deighton, 1851.

Harnack, A. von. *The Mission and Expansion of Christianity in the First Three Centuries.* Translated and edited by J. Moffatt.

2d ed. 2 vols. London and New York: Williams and Norgate, 1908.

_____. *Porphyrius 'Gegen die Christen', 15 Bücher: Zeugnisse, Fragmente und Referate.* APAW.PH 1. Berlin: Königlich Akademie der Wissenschaften, in Kommission bei Georg Reimer, 1916.

Heid, S. *Kreuz–Jerusalem–Kosmos: Aspekte frühchristlicher Staurologie.* JAC.E 31. Münster: Aschendorff, 2001.

Heinz, A. 'Ars celebrandi: Überlegungen zur Kunst, die Liturgie der Kirche zu feiern'. *Questions Liturgiques* 83 (2002): 107–26.

Henner, J. *Fragmenta Liturgica Coptica: Editionen und Kommentar liturgischer Texte der Koptischen Kirche des ersten Jahrtausends.* Studien und Texte zu Antike und Christentum 5. Tübingen: Mohr Siebeck, 2000.

Hoff, J. 'Das Verschwinden des Körpers: Eine Kritik an der "Wut des Verstehens" in der Liturgie'. *HerKor* 54 (2000): 149–55.

Hollerweger, H. *Die Reform des Gottesdienstes zur Zeit des Josephinismus in Österreich.* StPaLi 1. Regensburg: Pustet, 1976.

Jacobsen, W. 'Altarraum und Heiligengrab als liturgisches Konzept in der Auseinandersetzung des Nordens mit Rom'. In *Kunst und Liturgie im Mittelalter: Akten des internationalen Kongresses der Bibliotheca Hertziana und des Nederlands Instituut te Rome, Rom, 28.–30. September 1997*, edited by N. Bock, S. de Blaauw, C. L. Frommel, and H. Kessler, 65–74. RJ, supplement to vol. 33 (1999/2000). Munich: Hirmer, 2000.

_____. 'Organisationsformen des Sanktuariums im spätantiken und mittelalterlichen Kirchenbau: Wechselwirkungen von Altarraum und Liturgie aus kunsthistorischer Perspektive'. In *Kölnische Liturgie und ihre Geschichte: Studien zur interdisziplinären Erforschung des Gottesdienstes im*

Erzbistum Köln, edited by A. Gerhards and A. Odenthal, 67–97. LWQF 87. Münster: Aschendorff, 2000.

John Paul II. Encyclical Letter *Ecclesia de Eucharistia*. Vatican City: Libreria Editrice Vaticana, 2003.

Jungmann, J. A. *Liturgisches Erbe und pastorale Gegenwart: Studien und Vorträge*. Innsbruck: Tyrolia, 1960.

———. *The Mass of the Roman Rite: Its Origins and Development (Missarum Sollemnia)*. Translated by F. A. Brunner. 2 vols. New York: Benziger Brothers, 1951 and 1955.

———. *Messe im Gottesvolk: Ein nachkonziliarer Durchblick durch Missarum Sollemnia*. Freiburg: Herder, 1970.

———. *Missarum Sollemnia: Eine genetische Erklärung der römischen Messe*. 5th ed. 2 vols. Vienna: Herder, 1962.

———. 'Der neue Altar'. *Der Seelsorger* 37 (1967): 374–81.

———. Review of O. Nußbaum, *Der Standort des Liturgen am christlichen Altar vor dem Jahre 1000*. Bonn: Hanstein, 1965. *ZKTh* 88 (1966): 445–50.

Kaschewsky, R. 'Eine wichtige Veröffentlichung zur Zelebration *versus populum*'. *UVK* 30 (2000): 310–11.

Keller, E. *Eucharistie und Parusie: Liturgie- und theologiegeschichtliche Untersuchungen zur eschatologischen Dimension der Eucharistie anhand ausgewählter Zeugnisse aus frühkirchlicher und patristischer Zeit*. SF NF 70. Fribourg: Universitätsverlag, 1989.

Kidd, B. J. *Documents Illustrative of the Continental Reformation*. Oxford: Clarendon Press, 1911.

Kleinheyer, B. *Sakramentliche Feiern I: Die Feiern der Eingliederung in die Kirche*. GdK 7/1. Regensburg: Pustet, 1989.

Klöckener, M. 'Die Bedeutung der neu entdeckten Augustinus-Predigten (*Sermones Dolbeau*) für die liturgiegeschichtliche Forschung'. In *Augustin Prédicateur (395–411): Actes du Colloque International de Chantilly (5–7 septembre 1996)*, edited by G. Madec, 129–70. Collection des Études Augustiniennes, Série Antiquité 159. Paris: Institut d'Études Augustiniennes, 1998.

———. 'Conuersi ad dominum'. *AugL* 1 (1994): 1280–82.

Klötzl, G. '"Zwingende liturgische Notwendigkeit" zu Altarraumumbauten? Bemerkungen zu § 5 Absatz 4 Denkmalschutzgesetz'. *ÖZKD* 46 (1992): 38–43.

Korol, D. 'Neues zur Geschichte der verehrten Gräber und des zentralen Bezirks des Pilgerheiligtums in Cimitile-Nola'. *JAC* 35 (1992): 83–118.

Kraeling, C. H. *The Christian Building*. The Excavations at Dura-Europos. Final Report 8, pt. 2. New Haven: Dura-Europos Publications, 1967.

Krautheimer, R., with S. Ćurčić. *Early Christian and Byzantine Architecture*. 4th ed. New Haven and London: Yale University Press, 1986.

Kretschmar, G. 'Festkalender und Memorialstätten Jerusalems in altkirchlicher Zeit'. *ZDPV* 87 (1971): 167–205.

Kunzler, M. 'La liturgia all'inizio del Terzo Millennio'. In *Il Concilio Vaticano II: Recezione e attualità alla luce del Giubileo*, edited by R. Fisichella, 217–31. Milan: San Paolo, 2000.

Landsberger, F. 'The Sacred Direction in Synagogue and Church'. *HUCA* 28 (1957): 181–203.

Lang, U. M. 'Conversi ad Dominum: Zu Gebetsostung, Stellung des Liturgen am Altar und Kirchenbau'. *FKTh* 16 (2000): 81–123.

Lara, J. 'Versus Populum Revisited'. *Worship* 68 (1994): 210–21.

Lassus, J. 'La Liturgie dans les basiliques syriennes'. In *Atti dell' VIII Congresso internazionale di studi bizantini: Palermo 3–10 aprile 1951*, 418–28. Studi bizantini e neoellenici 8. Rome: Associazione nazionale per gli studi bizantini, 1953.

———. *Sanctuaires chrétiens de Syrie*. Paris: P. Geuthner, 1947.

Legg, J. W., ed. *Tracts on the Mass*. HBS 27. London: Harrison, 1904.

Lercaro, G. 'L'Heureux Développement'. *Not* 2 (1966): 157–61.

Lora, E., ed. *Enchiridion Vaticanum 15: Documenti ufficiali della Santa Sede 1996*. Bologna: Dehoniane, 1999.

Lorenzer, A. *Das Konzil der Buchhalter: Die Zerstörung der Sinnlichkeit: Eine Religionskritik*. Unabridged edition. Frankfurt am Main: Fischer-Taschenbuch-Verlag, 1984.

———. '"Sacrosanctum Concilium": Der Anfang der "Buchhalterei": Betrachtungen aus psychoanalytisch-kulturkritischer Sicht'. In *Gottesdienst–Kirche–Gesellschaft: Interdisziplinäre und ökumenische Standortbestimmungen nach 25 Jahren Liturgiereform*, edited by H. Becker, B. J. Hilberath, and U. Willers, 153–61. PiLi 5. St. Ottilien: EOS-Verlag, 1991.

Louth, A. *St John Damascene: Tradition and Originality in Byzantine Theology*. Oxford Early Christian Studies. Oxford: Oxford University Press, 2002.

Lubac, H. de. *The Splendor of the Church*. Translated by M. Mason. San Francisco: Ignatius Press, 1999.

Macquarrie, J. 'Subjectivity and Objectivity in Theology and Worship'. *Worship* 41 (1967): 152–60.

Mathews, T. F. 'An Early Roman Chancel Arrangement'. *RivAC* 38 (1962): 73–96.

Mayer-Himmelheber, S. *Bischöfliche Kunstpolitik nach dem Tridentinum: Der Secunda-Roma-Anspruch Carlo Borromeos und die mailändischen Verordnungen zu Bau und Ausstattung von Kirchen*. Munich: Tuduv-Verlagsgesellschaft, 1984.

Meßner, R. *Einführung in die Liturgiewissenschaft*. UTB 2173. Paderborn: Schöningh, 2001.

———. 'Probleme des eucharistischen Hochgebets'. In *Bewahren und Erneuern: Studien zur Meßliturgie: Festschrift für*

Hans Bernhard Meyer SJ zum 70. Geburtstag, edited by R. Meßner, E. Nagel, and R. Pacik, 174–201. IThS 42. Innsbruck and Vienna: Tyrolia, 1995.

———. 'Unterschiedliche Konzeptionen des Meßopfers im Spiegel von Bedeutung und Deutung der Interzessionen des römischen Canon missae'. In *Das Opfer: Biblischer Anspruch und liturgische Gestalt*, edited by A. Gerhards and K. Richter, 128–84. QD 186. Freiburg: Herder, 2000.

Metzger, M. 'La Place des liturges à l'autel'. *RevSR* 45 (1971): 113–45.

Meyer, H. B. *Luther und die Messe: Eine liturgiewissenschaftliche Untersuchung über das Verhältnis Luthers zum Meßwesen des späten Mittelalters*. KKTS 11. Paderborn: Bonifacius-Druckerei, 1965.

Michel, A. *Les Églises d'époque byzantine et ummayyade de la Jordanie (provinces d'Arabie et de Palestine), Vᵉ–VIIIᵉ siècle: Typologie architecturale et aménagements liturgiques (avec catalogue des monuments)*. Bibliothèque de l'antiquité tardive 2. Turnhout: Brepols, 2001.

Mingana, A. *The Apology of Timothy the Patriarch before the Caliph Mahdi*. Wood St, vol. 2, 1. Cambridge: W. Heffer and Sons, 1928.

Missale Romanum ex decreto Sacrosancti Oecumenici Concilii Vaticani II instauratum auctoritate Pauli PP. VI promulgatum. Editio typica. Vatican City: Typis Polyglottis Vaticanis, 1970.

Missale Romanum ex decreto Sacrosancti Oecumenici Concilii Vaticani II instauratum auctoritate Pauli PP. VI promulgatum Ioannis Pauli PP. II cura recognitum. Editio typica tertia. Vatican City: Typis Vaticanis, 2002.

Moll, H. *Die Lehre von der Eucharistie als Opfer: Eine dogmengeschichtliche Untersuchung vom Neuen Testament bis Irenäus von Lyon*. Theoph 26. Cologne: Hanstein, 1975.

Monnot, G. 'Salāt'. In *Encyclopédie de l'Islam*, edited by C. E. Bosworth, E. van Donzel, B. Lewis, and C. Pellat, 8:956–65. New edition. Leiden and Paris: Brill, 1995.

Moreton, M. J. 'Εἰς ἀνατολὰς βλέψατε: Orientation as a Liturgical Principle'. *StPatr* 18 (1982): 575–90.

Napier, C. 'The Altar in the Contemporary Church'. *CleR* 57 (1972): 624–32.

Nebel, J. 'Die *editio typica tertia* des *Missale Romanum*: Eine Untersuchung über die Veränderungen'. *Ecclesia Orans* 19 (2002): 265–314.

———. *Die Entwicklung des römischen Meßritus im ersten Jahrtausend anhand der* Ordines Romani: *Eine synoptische Darstellung*. Doctoral diss., Pontificium Athenaeum S. Anselmi de Urbe, 1998.

Neunheuser, B. 'Eucharistiefeier am Altare *versus populum*: Geschichte und Problematik'. In *Florentissima proles Ecclesiae: Miscellanea hagiographica, historica et liturgica Reginaldo Grégoire O.S.B. XII lustra complenti oblata*, edited by D. Gobbi, 417–44. Trento: Civis, 1996.

Newman, J. H. *Apologia pro Vita Sua*. London: Longman, Green, Longman, Roberts and Green, 1864.

———. *An Essay on the Development of Christian Doctrine*. New edition. London: Basil Montagu Pickering, 1878.

———. *The Via Media of the Anglican Church*. 2 vols. London: Basil Montagu Pickering, 1877.

Nichols, A. *Looking at the Liturgy: A Critical View of Its Contemporary Form*. San Francisco: Ignatius Press, 1996.

Nilgen, U. 'Die Bilder über dem Altar: Triumph- und Apsisbogenprogramme in Rom und Mittelitalien und ihr Bezug zur Liturgie'. In *Kunst und Liturgie im Mittelalter: Akten des internationalen Kongresses der Bibliotheca Hertziana und des Nederlands Instituut te Rome, Rom, 28.–30. September 1997*, edited by N. Bock, S. de Blaauw, C. L. Frommel, and H. Kessler, 75–89. RJ, supplement to vol. 33 (1999/2000). Munich: Hirmer, 2000.

Nußbaum, O. *Der Standort des Liturgen am christlichen Altar vor dem Jahre 1000: Eine archäologische und liturgiegeschichtliche Untersuchung.* Theoph 18. 2 vols. Bonn: Hanstein, 1965.

———. 'Die Zelebration versus populum und der Opfercharakter der Messe'. *ZKTh* 93 (1971): 148–67.

Odenthal, A. 'Denkmalpflege als Postulat der Liturgiereform'. *LJ* 42 (1992): 249–59.

Pallath, P., ed. *La liturgia eucaristica della chiesa siro-malabarese.* Quaderni di Rivista Liturgica 1. Padua: Edizioni Messagero, 2000.

Peeters, C. J. A. C. *De liturgische dispositie van het vroegchristelijk kerkgebouw: Samenhang van cathedra, leesplaats en altaar in de basiliek van de vierde tot de zevende eeuw.* Assen: Van Gorcum, 1969.

Peterson, E. *Frühkirche, Judentum und Gnosis: Studien und Untersuchungen.* Freiburg: Herder, 1959.

Pietri, C. *Roma christiana: Recherches sur l'Église de Rome, son organisation, sa politique, son idéologie de Miltiade à Sixte III (311–440).* 2 vols. BEFAR 224. Rome: École française de Rome, 1976.

Pius XII. *Littera Encyclicae de Sacra Liturgia 'Mediator Dei'. AAS* 39 (1947): 521–95.

Podossinov, A. 'Himmelsrichtung (kultische)'. *RAC* 15 (1991): 233–86.

Ratzinger, J. 'Catholicism after the Council'. Translated by P. Russell. *The Furrow* 18 (1967): 3–23.

———. '*L'Esprit de la liturgie* ou la fidelité au Concile: Réponse au Père Gy'. *La Maison-Dieu* 230 (2002): 114–20.

———. *The Feast of Faith: Approaches to a Theology of the Liturgy.* Translated by G. Harrison. San Francisco: Ignatius Press, 1986.

_____. *The Spirit of the Liturgy.* Translated by J. Saward. San Francisco: Ignatius Press, 2000.

_____. 'Theologie der Liturgie'. *FKTh* 18 (2002): 1–13.

Ratzinger, J. with V. Messori. *The Ratzinger Report: An Exclusive Interview on the State of the Church.* Translated by S. Attanasio and G. Harrison. San Francisco: Ignatius Press, 1985.

Renhart, E. *Das syrische Bema: Liturgisch-archäologische Untersuchungen.* GrTS 20. Graz: Schnider, 1995.

Rennings, H., and M. Klöckener, eds. *Dokumente zur Erneuerung der Liturgie.* Vol. 1, *Dokumente des Apostolischen Stuhls 1963–1973.* Kevelaer: Butzon and Bercker, 1983.

Righetti, M. *Manuale di storia liturgica.* Vol. 1, *Introduzione generale.* 3d ed. Milan: Editrice Ancora, 1964.

Rouwhorst, G. 'Jewish Liturgical Traditions in Early Syriac Christianity'. *VigChr* 51 (1997): 72–93.

Sacra Congregatio Rituum. *Instructio ad exsecutionem Constitutionis de sacra Liturgia recte ordinandam 'Inter Oecumenici'.* *AAS* 56 (1964): 877–900.

Savon, H. 'Zacharie 6, 12, et les justifications patristiques de la prière vers l'orient'. In *Ecclesia orans: Mélanges patristiques offerts au Père Adalbert G. Hamman, O.F.M.*, edited by V. Saxer [= *Aug* 20 (1980):], 319–33.

Schönborn, C. *Loving the Church: Spiritual Exercises Preached in the Presence of Pope John Paul II.* Translated by J. Saward. San Francisco: Ignatius Press, 1998.

Schreiter, R. J. *Constructing Local Theologies.* London: SCM, 1985.

Schulz, F. 'Das Mahl der Brüder: Herrenmahl in neuer Gestalt'. *JLH* 15 (1970): 32–51.

Seager, A. R. 'Ancient Synagogue Architecture: An Overview'. In *Ancient Synagogues: The State of Research*, edited by J. Gutmann, 39–47. BJSt 22. Chico, Calif.: Scholars Press, 1981.

_____. 'The Architecture of the Dura and Sardis Synagogues'. In *The Dura-Europos Synagogue: A Re-evaluation (1932–1972)*, edited by J. Gutmann, 79–116. Missoula, Mont.: University of Montana, 1973.

Selhorst, H. *Die Platzordnungen im Gläubigenraum der altchristlichen Kirche.* Münster: Aschendorff, 1931.

Siebel, W. *Liturgie als Angebot: Bemerkungen aus soziologischer Sicht.* Berlin: Morus-Verlag, 1972.

Sodi, M., and A. M. Triacca, eds. *Missale Romanum: Editio Princeps (1570).* Monumenta Liturgica Concilii Tridentini 2. Vatican City: Libreria Editrice Vaticana, 1998.

Spinks, B. D. 'Eucharistic Offering in the East Syrian Anaphoras'. *OCP* 50 (1984): 347–71.

Steck, W. *Der Liturgiker Amalarius: Eine quellenkritische Untersuchung zu Leben und Werk eines Theologen der Karolingerzeit.* MThS.H 35. St. Ottilien: EOS-Verlag, 2000.

Steiner, J. *Liturgiereform in der Aufklärungszeit: Eine Darstellung am Beispiel Vitus Anton Winters.* FThSt 100. Freiburg: Herder, 1976.

Stevenson, K. *Eucharist and Offering.* New York: Pueblo, 1986.

Stock, A. 'Gotteshaus und Kirchgang'. *LJ* 39 (1989): 5–18.

Taft, R. F. 'The Dialogue before the Anaphora in the Byzantine Eucharistic Liturgy. II: The *Sursum corda*'. *OCP* 54 (1988): 47–77.

_____. 'Some Notes on the Bema in the East and West Syrian Traditions'. *OCP* 34 (1968): 326–59. Reprint with supplementary notes in R. F. Taft. *Liturgy in Byzantium and Beyond.* CStS 493. Aldershot: Ashgate, 1995.

_____. 'Textual Problems in the Diaconal Admonition before the Anaphora in the Byzantine Tradition'. *OCP* 49 (1983): 340–65.

Taylor, J. G. *Yahweh and the Sun: Biblical and Archaeological Evidence for Sun Worship in Ancient Israel.* JSOT, supplement 111. Sheffield: JSOT Press, 1993.

Tchalenko, G. *Églises syriennes à bêma.* Paris: P. Geuthner, 1990.

———. *Villages antiques de la Syrie du Nord: Le Massif du Bélus à l'époque romaine.* 3 vols. Paris: P. Geuthner, 1953–1958.

Tchalenko, G., and E. Baccache. *Églises de village de la Syrie du Nord.* 2 vols. Paris: P. Geuthner, 1979–1980.

Thümmel, H. G. 'Versammlungsraum, Kirche, Tempel'. In *Gemeinde ohne Tempel / Community without Temple: Zur Substituierung und Transformation des Jerusalemer Tempels und seines Kults im Alten Testament, antiken Judentum und frühen Christentum,* edited by B. Ego, A. Lange, P. Pilhofer, K. Ehlers, 489–504. WUNT 118. Tübingen: Mohr Siebeck, 1999.

Thurian, M. 'La Liturgie, contemplation du mystère'. *Not* 32 (1996): 690–97.

Tongeren, L. van. 'Vers une utilisation dynamique et flexible de l'espace: Une réflexion renouvelée sur le réaménagement d'églises'. *Questions Liturgiques* 83 (2002): 156–78.

Torevell, D. *Losing the Sacred: Ritual, Modernity and Liturgical Reform.* Edinburgh: T and T Clark, 2000.

Toynbee, J., and J. Ward Perkins. *The Shrine of St. Peter and the Vatican Excavations.* London: Longmans, Green, 1956.

Trapp, W. *Vorgeschichte und Ursprung der liturgischen Bewegung vorwiegend in Hinsicht auf das deutsche Sprachgebiet.* 1940. Reprint, Münster: Antiquariat Stenderhoff, 1979.

Ulevičius, B. *Dieviškieji Rytai: Povatikaninė liturginė reforma ir 'altorių atgręžimo' klausimas.* Vilnius: Aidai, 2002.

Vazheeparampil, P. *The Making and Unmaking of Tradition: Towards a Theology of the Liturgical Renewal in the Syro-Malabar Church.* Rome: Mar Thoma Yogam, 1998.

Voelker, E. C. *Charles Borromeo's* Instructiones Fabricae et Supellectilis Ecclesiasticae, *1577: A Translation with Commentary and Analysis.* Ph.D. diss., Syracuse University, 1977.

Vööbus, A. 'New Light on the Text of the Canons in the Doctrine of Addai'. *Journal of the Syriac Academy* 1 (1975): 3–21.

Vogel, C. 'La Croix eschatologique'. In A. M. Dubarle et al., *Noël, Épiphanie, retour du Christ,* 85–108. Lex orandi 40. Paris: Éditions du Cerf, 1967.

_____. 'L'Orientation vers l'Est du célébrant et des fidèles pendant la célébration eucharistique'. *OrSyr* 9 (1964): 3–37.

_____. 'Sol aequinoctialis: Problèmes et technique de l'orientation dans le culte chrétien'. *RevSR* 36 (1962): 175–211.

_____. 'Versus ad Orientem: L'Orientation dans les *Ordines romani* du haut moyen age'. *StMed* 3/1 (1960): 447–69.

Vries, W. de. *Die Sakramententheologie bei den Nestorianern.* OCA 133. Rome: Pontificium Institutum Orientalium Studiorum, 1947.

_____. *Die Sakramententheologie bei den syrischen Monophysiten.* OCA 125. Rome: Pontificium Institutum Orientalium Studiorum, 1940.

Wallraff, M. *Christus verus sol: Sonnenverehrung und Christentum in der Spätantike.* JAC.E 32. Münster: Aschendorff, 2001.

_____. 'La preghiera verso l'oriente: Alle origini di un uso liturgico'. In *La preghiera nel tardo antico: Dalle origini a Sant' Agostino. XXVII Incontro di studiosi dell' antichità cristiana. Roma, 7–9 maggio 1998,* 463–69. SEAug 66. Rome: Institutum Patristicum Augustinanum, 1999.

_____. 'Die Ursprünge der christlichen Gebetsostung'. *ZKG* 111 (2000): 169–84.

Walther, V. '"Celebratio versus populum": Evangelisches Echo und Fragen an den evangelischen Gottesdienst'. *HlD* 53 (1999): 137–42.

Ward-Perkins, J. B. 'The Shrine of St. Peter and Its Twelve Spiral Columns'. In *Studies in Roman and Early Christian Architecture*, 469–88. London: Pindar Press, 1994.

Weigand, E. 'Die Ostung in der frühchristlichen Architektur: Neue Tatsachen zu einer alten Problemfrage'. In *Festschrift Sebastian Merkle*, edited by W. Schellberg, 370–85. Düsseldorf: Schwann, 1922.

Wensinck, A. J. 'Kibla I'. In *Encyclopédie de L'Islam*, edited by C. E. Bosworth, E. van Donzel, B. Lewis, and C. Pellat, 5:84–85. New edition. Leiden and Paris: Brill, 1986.

Wilkinson, J. 'Orientation, Jewish and Christian'. *PEQ* 116 (1984): 16–30.

Williams, R. *Eucharistic Sacrifice: The Roots of a Metaphor*. GLS 31. Bramcote: Grove Books, 1982.

Willis, G. G. *A History of Early Roman Liturgy to the Death of Pope Gregory the Great*. With a memoir of G. G. Willis by M. Moreton. HBS, Subsidia 1. London: Boydell Press, 1994.

Witakowski, W. 'The Origin of the "Teaching of the Apostles"'. In *IV Symposium Syriacum 1984*, 161–71. OCA 229. Rome: Pontificium Institutum Studiorum Orientalium, 1987.

INDEX